WRITING MEANINGFUL
EVALUATIONS *for*
Non-Instructional Staff
—— RIGHT NOW!!

WRITING MEANINGFUL EVALUATIONS *for* Non-Instructional Staff — RIGHT NOW!!

The Principal's Quick-Start Reference Guide

Cornelius L. Barker
Claudette J. Searchwell

CORWIN PRESS
A Sage Publications Company
Thousand Oaks, California

For information:

Corwin Press
A Sage Publications Company
2455 Teller Road
Thousand Oaks, California 91320
www.corwinpress.com

Sage Publications Ltd.
6 Bonhill Street
London EC2A 4PU
United Kingdom

Sage Publications India Pvt. Ltd.
B-42, Panchsheel Enclave
Post Box 4109
New Delhi 110 017 India

Printed in the United States of America

Library of Congress Cataloging-in-Publication Data

Barker, Cornelius L.
Writing meaningful evaluations for non-instructional staff—right now!! : the principal's quick-start reference guide / Cornelius L. Barker, Claudette J. Searchwell.
        p. cm.
ISBN 0-7619-3980-6 (cloth) — ISBN 0-7619-3981-4 (pbk.)
    1. School employees—Rating of—Handbooks, manuals, etc. 2. School personnel management—Handbooks, manuals, etc. I. Searchwell, Claudette J. II. Title.
LB2831.57.E35B37 2004
371.2´02—dc22

                            2003021566

This book is printed on acid-free paper.

             05   06   07   10   9   8   7   6   5   4   3   2

Acquisitions editor:	Robb Clouse
Editorial assistant:	Jingle Vea
Production editor:	Sanford Robinson
Copy editor:	Teresa Herlinger
Typesetter:	C&M Digitals (P) Ltd.
Proofreader:	Eileen Delaney
Cover designer:	Michael Dubowe

CONTENTS

PREFACE

Writing Meaningful Evaluations for Non-Instructional Staff—Right Now!! was conceived as a natural extension of its partner guides, *Writing Meaningful Teacher Evaluations—Right Now!!* and *Writing Year-End Teacher Improvement Plans—Right Now!!*

While the teaching staff is clearly responsible for the delivery of instruction in the classroom, laboratory, and/or resource center, the educational process unfolds outside of those confines as well. An ever-growing number of adjunct and support personnel share responsibilities for the delivery of a full range of student services, geared to ensure the academic, social, physical, and emotional growth of each child. This phenomenon is true of all schools, whether located in urban, suburban, or rural school districts.

Writing Meaningful Evaluations for Non-Instructional Staff—Right Now!! offers the busy administrator instant job description information and a compendium of statements specific to the function of *staff members who do not deliver instruction.* This stipulation points to the relatedness of the job titles included in this guide. Without the services of the staff outlined in this guide, no school could, or would, attempt to function.

Five performance areas list benchmark skills relevant to each job title. Although the required tasks vary widely, universal elements exist in the rubrics used to judge their performance:

A. *Specific Tasks.* This benchmark outlines job description duties and conditions that are generally considered to be basic to the position. Judgment on the quality of performance could reasonably be based on successful completion of the competencies listed under this heading.

B. *Level of Expertise.* What competencies and/or skills, above those that are considered standard for qualification for the position and successful fulfillment of job performance, does the staff member possess?

C. *Preparation and Organization.* This benchmark points to the procedures that are used by the staff member in order to perform tasks at a peak level of efficiency and productivity.

D. *Related Responsibilities.* Other than the basic duties associated with the job, what additional related tasks are performed? What creative, innovative, and/or supplementary tasks does the staff member perform or offer as his/her contribution to the school organization?

E. *Interpersonal Domain.* One of the key elements of a successful school is the spirit of teamwork that stimulates both staff and students to succeed. This benchmark looks at the contribution the staff member makes to the overall climate of collegiality, mutual respect, and cooperation shared among staff, students, parents, and the community.

Writing Meaningful Evaluations for Non-Instructional Staff—Right Now!! relieves the administrator of finding just the right word to use when assessing the performance of non-instructional staff.

At last, the final element in the array of unique, practical, and much sought-after guides that facilitate the professional, comprehensive, and personalized assessment of staff—completed easily, and on time!!

ABOUT THE AUTHORS

Cornelius L. Barker is a much sought-after lecturer for school and community groups on the subject of current cognitive and behavioral trends exhibited by today's youth. His career in education has spanned more than 25 years in the capacity of classroom teacher and administrator on both the elementary and secondary levels.

He is currently serving as a building administrator in a large secondary school.

Claudette J. Searchwell is a retired elementary school principal whose career spanned 34 years in the public schools. Her service in the field of education included posts as classroom teacher, assistant director of a federal basic skills program, coordinator of citywide after-school and summer programs, assistant principal, and principal.

She is currently a member of the adjunct staff at Kean University, Union, New Jersey, serving as supervisor of pre-certification students completing their senior internship.

INTRODUCTION

School administrators have a mandate to provide comprehensive educational services in a safe and productive environment. They can only accomplish this with the aid of dedicated and well-trained instructional and non-instructional staff.

The concept of developing a guide that addresses the specific need of creating performance assessments for non-instructional school personnel was long overdue. In this guide, we recognize the important role played by *staff who do not share the day-to-day responsibilities of providing instruction in the classroom,* but who contribute valuable services to students and to the smooth operation of the school.

Staff members within the school organization must be evaluated. This certainly includes *non-instructional personnel, defined in this guide as those who do not have responsibility for working with a fixed group of students for the entire school year.* In most instances, formal evaluations are required. Where this does not apply, as with volunteers, informal assessments are still required, along with letters of recommendation, reports, and data collection geared toward quantifying and qualifying the delivery of services.

This guide simplifies those tasks for the busy administrator.

Sections I through VIII provide the performance statements for staff—Administration through Security—under five benchmark areas.

Suggested "Pats on the Back," a breakthrough addition first used in *Writing Meaningful Teacher Evaluations—Right Now!!* reappears here and can be found after each major section in the non-instructional guide.

The "Evaluation Organizer," an innovative tool on which observed classroom practices can be recorded, allows the busy administrator to easily transcribe brief notations into in-depth statements.

Duplicate the page entitled "Record of Evaluations" and keep an accurate account of your progress as you conduct informal observations and complete formal evaluations and pre/post conferences.

Duplicate the "Checklist of Basic Documentation and/or Conditions" and take a copy with you as you visit instructional areas when conducting both informal and formal evaluation visitations.

A summary statement for each of the job titles included in the Guide can be found in the "Description of Positions" and used for ready reference.

The proliferation of job titles in the schools has resulted in an ever-increasing workload for building administrators. This guide is a "must-have" for educators charged with the responsibility of delivering comprehensive, professional staff assessments. This, along with its partner guide, *Writing Meaningful Teacher Evaluations—Right Now!!* will simplify that task, quickly and easily, for *most job titles within the school organization!*

Part I

WRITING THE EVALUATION

Includes performance statements and suggested "pats on the back" for

- ✏ Section I   Aides

- ✏ Section II   Clerical Staff

- ✏ Section III   Counselors

- ✏ Section IV   Disciplinarians

- ✏ Section V   Health/Medical Personnel

- ✏ Section VI   Maintenance Personnel

- ✏ Section VII Security Staff

- ✏ Section VIII Administration

Performance statements in each section include

A. Specific Tasks

B. Level of Expertise

C. Preparation and Organization

D. Related Duties

E. Interpersonal Domain

Section I

AIDES

Paraprofessional, Teacher Aide, Teacher Assistant

This section assists the administrator in determining if basic qualifications, expertise, and requirements for successful fulfillment of duties inherent to the job title have been demonstrated.

Performance Statements

Note: With occasional editing, Performance Statements are interchangeable between job titles in this section, when appropriate.

A. Specific Tasks
   a. Is knowledgeable of (physical, behavioral, learning) disabilities of (specific students, class, group).
   b. Provides direct aid to (classroom teacher, student with disability).
   c. Reports directly to the (administrator, classroom teacher, department head).
   d. Provides assistance to (individual student, small group, class) under the direction of the classroom teacher.
   e. (Sets up, Maintains, Arranges, Readies) (laboratory, classroom, learning center, audiovisual, computerized) (materials, areas, equipment).
   f. Upholds standard classroom procedures.
   g. Consistently maintains (rules and regulations, behavior modification strategies, class and school code of conduct, etc.).
   h. (Collects, Checks for completeness of, Collates, etc.) (homework, reports, collections, forms, notes, etc.) from students under the direction of the classroom teacher.
   i. Assists with monitoring the progress of students engaged in (seatwork, hands-on activities, experiments, projects, etc.).
   j. Under the direction of the classroom teacher, (collects, edits, records, distributes, etc.) (standardized, informal, unit, chapter) tests and quizzes.

B. Level of Expertise
  a. Demonstrates creative talents through (decorating classroom, constructing bulletin boards, developing learning/teaching aids).
  b. (Corrects, Records) student assessment documents under the direction of the classroom teacher.
  c. Is knowledgeable in the use of (audiovisuals, technology, software) used in the classroom.
  d. Possesses (exemplary, exceptional, etc.) (musical, dance, creative, academic, oratory, writing, etc.) talents.
  e. Performs clerical duties related to classroom function, including (typing, word processing, taking attendance, duplicating materials, record keeping, etc.).
  f. Demonstrates expertise in the use of higher-order (technological, electronic, manual recording and informational) (systems, equipment) related to duties.
  g. Maintains accurate, neat, and timely records and files.
  h. Is knowledgeable of all cognitive, emotional, social, and physical disabilities of the (student, group, class) to which he or she is assigned.
  i. (Upholds, Carries out, Implements, Reinforces) (classroom, school, district, IEP) behavior modification strategies.
  j. Demonstrates (familiarity with, knowledge of) curriculum and uses this knowledge to assist students with classroom work.

C. Preparation and Organization
  a. Assumes responsibility for maintenance of (teacher's, students') work area.
  b. (Sets up, Prepares, Maintains, etc.) audiovisual equipment.
  c. Prepares student supplies and equipment.
  d. Is prompt and reliable in reporting to assigned duty area.
  e. Maintains an excellent record of (attendance, punctuality).
  f. (Selects, Gathers, etc.) supplementary reading material for classroom use.
  g. Inventories and manages classroom supplies and equipment.
  h. Participates in (school, district, union-related) training courses in order to (upgrade, enhance, acquire) skills.
  i. Maintains an (appropriate, professional) (appearance, demeanor, manner).
  j. Accepts constructive (suggestions, criticism, direction) with grace, maturity, and professionalism.

D. Related Duties
  a. Maintains (classroom, corridor) bulletin boards.
  b. Accompanies students to (lunchroom, special subject areas, lavatories, playground, assembly, buses, etc.).
  c. Participates in classroom activity (periods, projects, etc.).

d. Demonstrates flexibility in response to (requests, changes, assigned duties, stressful situations, etc.).

e. Monitors students for brief periods during absence of teacher.

f. Arranges, monitors, and participates in (indoor, classroom, playground, outdoor) games and/or activities.

g. Assists students who are (absent, ill, transferred in or out) with (remedial, catch-up, missed, current) classroom work.

h. Monitors students during (field trips, intraclass activities, assemblies, etc.).

i. (Prepares, Operates, Maintains) (ambulatory, orthopedic, learning) (aids, devices) required for students with disabilities.

j. (Volunteers for, Participates in) special school activities including (fundraising, PTA, Back-to-School Night, etc.) events.

E. Interpersonal Domain

a. (Works well with, Collaborates with) (teacher, colleagues, staff, administration, etc.) in the performance of duties.

b. Assists in maintaining a neat and orderly classroom (assigned area, physical plant).

c. Refers (suggestions, inquiries, comments, etc.) related to students to the classroom teacher.

d. Performs (classroom-, school-) delegated duties with (exceptional, sound, acceptable) level of expertise.

e. (Forges, Enjoys) a personal relationship of (responsibility, compassion, caring, fondness, etc.) with disabled students assigned to his or her care.

f. Explores opportunities to (participate, enroll, engage) in (continuing education, college courses, training sessions, etc.).

g. Communicates via (telephone, note or letter, visiting the home, e-mail, automatic messaging device, etc.) with parents on issues related to student progress, under the direction of the classroom teacher.

h. Prepares (notices, memorandums, fliers, bulletins, invitations) (announcing, promoting) school (field trips, social events, sports, meetings, conferences) to be sent to parents.

i. Assists in maintaining safety, behavior, decorum, and order in common areas, including the (cafeteria, playground, corridors, study halls, gymnasium, auditorium, locker rooms, detention rooms).

j. Demonstrates support for (school, students, district) through attendance at school-related (activities, sports events, concerts, shows, fundraising events).

Suggested "Pats on the Back"

This section is geared to provide you with ideas for choosing just the right words to applaud exemplary performance. We hope you will have cause to make liberal use of these "pats on the back."

1. You provide our students with the (personal instruction, personal attention, remedial assistance) that they need. Our teachers appreciate your efforts.

2. The personalized service you provide to your special-needs students is without equal. In you, (he, she, they) (has, have) found an advocate and a friend.

3. You make a difference in the lives of children. Your work with our (insert grade level) graders is valuable and much appreciated.

4. We count on your dedicated and professional service in order to help our teachers provide equity in the delivery of instruction. Thank you for providing quality service to our students.

5. You have taken the initiative to remain current in the use of (technology in the classroom, audio-visual equipment, etc.). Thank you for your voluntary efforts toward professional development.

6. (Name of school) benefits from your decision to make becoming a (teacher aide or assistant, paraprofessional) your career choice. You are a valued member of the school family.

7. You (model, demonstrate) exceptional (creative talents, dedication to your position, concern for the students, reliability, job productivity, performance, etc.). Thank you for your excellent service.

8. You are to be commended for (meeting, surpassing) the new educational (standards, requirements) for your position. Your accomplishment is a testimony to your dedication and professionalism.

9. You demonstrate your acquired knowledge and your ability to productively assist our teachers and students on a daily basis. We count on your continued support and dedication.

10. You are adept in your knowledge of how best to assist students with (academic, learning, emotional) needs. Your efforts help them to maximize their potential for achieving success.

CLERICAL STAFF

Secretary, Supervisor Clerk, Clerk

This section assists the administrator in determining if basic qualifications, expertise, and requirements for successful fulfillment of duties inherent to the job title have been demonstrated.

Performance Statements

Note: With occasional editing, Performance Statements are interchangeable between job titles in this section, when appropriate.

A. Specific Tasks
    a. (Reviews, Checks, Corrects, Edits, Certifies) all work before finalizing.
    b. Prepares requisitions and maintains (follow-up, completion) records regarding disposition of requests.
    c. Accurately prepares meeting agendas.
    ✱ d. Answers and reroutes telephone calls.
    e. Checks all (reports, information, data) for accuracy.
    f. Compiles (statistical, personal, public relations, communication) data.
    g. Guides, instructs, and designs tasks for all subordinate clerical staff.
    ✱ h. Sorts and distributes correspondence.
    i. Prepares (weekly, monthly, periodic, summary, annual, etc.) (statements, reports, ledgers, etc.).
    j. Demonstrates the ability to (read, write, speak, understand, interpret, communicate) in (English, American Sign Language, Braille) sufficiently enough to perform all duties required of the position.

B. Level of Expertise
    ✱ a. Handles special requests with (competence, accuracy, grace, calm, cheerfulness, etc.).
    b. Is knowledgeable of and adheres to prescribed rules and regulations governing the position.

✳ c. (Handles, Expedites) multiple tasks with grace and competence.

✳ d. Assumes a major role in (performing, planning, revising, initiating) office routines and procedures.

e. Conducts independent research to support accuracy of (data, reports, compilations, etc.).

f. Maintains petty cash funds in the manner prescribed by (district, school, administration).

g. Is (conversant with, knowledgeable of, competent in using) all office-related software.

h. Is adept in the use of all office (technological, electronic, recording, communication, manual) equipment.

i. Maintains accurate record of personnel (attendance, tardiness, sick leave, vacation leave, health benefits, etc.).

j. Demonstrates the ability to perform all general and specialized tasks of clerical personnel.

C. Preparation and Organization

a. Prioritizes work assignments in order of (due date, importance, request, need, etc.).

b. Organizes workload into manageable tasks.

✳ c. Develops and implements effective work habits.

✳ d. (Maintains, Classifies, Indexes, Cross-references) records and files.

e. Enjoys excellent personal record of (attendance, punctuality).

f. Maintains a running record of office inventory of supplies and equipment.

g. Manages office petty cash fund for purchase, repair, and/or replenishment of office equipment.

h. (Communicates, Works) with vendors in order to expedite timely and cost-effective (purchases, rates).

✳ i. Streamlines office procedures to facilitate organization, performance, and user-friendly ambience.

✳ j. Maintains a professional demeanor, appearance, and work ethic.

D. Related Duties

✳ a. Relieves superior of nonessential (tasks, details, decision making, problem solving, interruptions, etc.).

✳ b. Represents the best interest of the school in conducting all (transactions, duties).

c. (Handles, Reviews, Accepts, etc.) complaints and aids in their timely resolution, whenever possible.

d. (Schedules, Conducts, Advertises for) (pre-interviews, interviews) of clerical candidates for employment.

✳ e. Is knowledgeable of and answers inquiries relative to all facets of the school organization.

f. Makes school announcements, under the direction of the building administrators.

      g. Maintains office equipment at peak operational level.

      h. Maintains an ongoing record of maintenance of office equipment.

✱ i. Serves as a liaison between the school and (other schools, the district office, agencies, community groups, etc.).

      j. Maintains office bulletin board in organized, accurate, and aesthetic manner.

E. Interpersonal Domain

✱ a. Maintains a user-friendly office environment.

✱ b. Represents (organization, school) well through (his, her) (appropriate, pleasing, professional, friendly) manner.

      c. Clearly articulates information relative to school (functions, personnel, location, etc.).

      d. Participates in school (cultural, social, community) events.

      e. Able to defuse (hostile, emergency, etc.) situations quickly and effectively.

      f. Attends (district, union, professional) training workshops in order to (upgrade, enhance, acquire, review) skills.

✱ g. Maintains a well-organized and aesthetic office space.

      h. Office is maintained in a well-aerated and temperature-controlled condition.

✱ i. (Directs, Redirects) requests made by visitors to office to correct (administrator, individual, department, student, etc.).

✱ j. Makes (school, office) a welcoming place to visit.

Suggested "Pats on the Back"

This section is geared to provide you with ideas for choosing just the right words to applaud exemplary performance. We hope you will have cause to make liberal use of these "pats on the back."

✱ 1. I often receive compliments about the "warmth" of the greetings visitors receive when entering the office. Thank you for making (name of school) a friendly place to visit.

✱ 2. Thank you for the efficient manner in which you maintain school records.

      3. My preparation for today's meeting gave testimony to the benefits of organization and readiness. Your efforts made that possible. Thank you!

      4. The consistent construction of professionally made (informational brochures, meeting agendas, monthly calendars, bulletins, notices to parents) enhances our school (public relations, communication efforts) by leaps and bounds! Thank you for your creativity and attention to detail when preparing them.

5. You are the hub that keeps the spokes of our school wheel in position. You are valued for the role you play.

6. Your technological ability is state-of-the-art. I applaud your expertise and the manner in which you utilize your special skills.

7. Dependability, dedication, and skill are hallmarks of the manner in which you perform your duty.

8. I have come to rely on your superior organizational skills to help propel me through the many tasks that must be accomplished each day. Please know that you are appreciated.

9. We count on your ability to (problem solve, compile data, field inquiries, soothe anxieties, ease concerns). You are needed—and appreciated.

10. It is clear that you have the best interests of the students and staff at heart from the manner in which you perform your duties. You are a valued member of the (name of school) team.

COUNSELORS

Child Study Team, Guidance, Attendance, Student Assistance

This section assists the administrator in determining if basic qualifications, expertise, and requirements for successful fulfillment of duties inherent to the job title have been demonstrated.

Performance Statements

Note: With occasional editing, Performance Statements are interchangeable between job titles in this section, when appropriate.

Child Study Team (CST) Counselor

A. Specific Tasks
   a. Conducts (individual, group, whole-class) counseling sessions.
   b. Confers with all staff who impact on student (progress, placement, disability).
   c. Aids student to make informed (educational, vocational, personal) decisions.
   d. Serves as a referral agent to (agencies, organizations, schools, programs) to promote students' best interests.
   e. Maintains student records that are current, accurate, and (constructed, formulated) in a manner that allows for their easy interpretation.
   f. Performs as an integral member of a team by providing (counseling, informational, student, community, placement, consultation, testing) services.
   g. Serves as an integral member of the school student referral team.
   h. Collaborates with classroom teachers on all matters of (social, emotional, academic, functional) importance to the classified student.

      i. Provides continuing (evaluative, diagnostic, advisory) assistance on all matters relative to (referred, classified) students.

      j. (Collaborates, Cooperates, Confers) with the classroom teacher regarding matters of classroom behavior and to formulate behavior modification strategies, where needed.

B. Level of Expertise

      a. (Monitors progress of, Offers insight into) strategies geared to support the progress of classified student in (regular education, mainstream, inclusion, self-contained) classroom settings.

      b. (Oversees, Monitors) classified students as they participate in (regular education, mainstreamed) activities.

      c. Serves as a resource person in specific area of expertise.

      d. Collaborates with professional staff to formulate (school, group, individualized) behavior modification strategies.

      e. Works with assigned team, as well as district professionals, to expedite caseloads.

      f. Collaborates with professional staff to construct schedules to assure classified students will receive all required services.

      g. Assists classroom teacher to interpret specific aspects of students' Individual Education Plans (IEP).

      h. Maintains anecdotal records on all (referred, classified) students.

      i. Contributes to the development of Individual Education Plans (IEPs) according to area of expertise.

      j. Collaborates with (classroom teacher, Child Study Team) regarding choice of appropriate (curriculum, materials, etc.) to be used by classified students.

C. Preparation and Organization

      a. Possesses academic and all other certification required for the position.

      b. Collaborates with (administration, teachers, specialists, etc.) regarding (strategies, programs, techniques) required to meet the specific needs of the students.

      c. Remains current with all available software germane to his or her field.

      d. Enjoys a (professional, high, exemplary) level of decision-making skills.

      e. Knowledgeable of current (theories, practices) in the field.

      f. Maintains a professional library relevant to the field of expertise.

      g. Effectively utilizes (appropriate, modern) technology in the performance of duties.

      h. Attends professional (workshops, conferences, etc.).

      i. Keeps (abreast of, current with) all district regulations and state laws relevant to the field.

      j. Utilizes the Internet to gain additional information regarding the field.

D. Related Duties
   a. Helps students to (understand, appreciate, utilize) their talents and (overcome, minimize) their disabilities.
   b. Assists students to acquire life skills.
   c. Collaborates with staff to coordinate efforts to ensure students opportunities to (maximize successes, develop competencies, realize their potential).
   d. Facilitates the smooth (transition, transfer, placement) of students.
   e. Represents the (district, school) on panels and/or at (workshops, conferences) at which services for students with disabilities are (explored, discussed).
   f. Maintains a pattern of timely response to (inquiries, requests, concerns) posed by (administrators, colleagues, parents, students).
   g. Assists (instructional staff, parents) to complete all required (forms, reports).
   h. (Assists, Guides) students in their efforts to formulate (vocational, employment, housing, further education, life) decisions.
   i. Collaborates with school guidance counselor on matters related to students with disabilities, e.g., achievement tests, etc.
   j. Renders services in area of expertise to students, regardless of sex, ethnicity, race, or disability.

E. Interpersonal Domain
   a. Works productively as a member of a professional team.
   b. Makes contact with parents to acquire information needed to (diagnose, place, provide services to) students with disabilities.
   c. Helps students to recognize and take responsibility for their (progress, actions, behavior).
   d. Proactive in efforts to communicate with (administrators, parents, staff) on matters pertaining to students with disabilities.
   e. Represents the (district, school) in area of expertise at (professional, community, religious, partnership, business, social) events.
   f. Makes contact with prospective (employers, vocational schools, housing agencies) and assists students to make (appropriate, informed) decisions regarding life choices.
   g. Helps parents (evaluate, develop, modify) home conditions in the light of providing the optimum environment for their children.
   h. Provides informational materials and consulting services to (parents, groups, colleagues, etc.).

   i. (Collaborates, Cooperates) with therapeutic specialists, including (speech clinicians, occupational therapy specialists, nurses, etc.).
   j. (Consistently seeks, Identifies) additional resources to enhance services offered to students, both inside and outside of the district.

Guidance Counselor

   A. Specific Tasks
      a. Possesses all prerequisite academic and other certificates required for the position and observes the highest ethical standards in the performance of duties.
      b. Provides counseling services for individual, group, or whole-class participants.
      c. (Assists, Counsels) students who demonstrate problems of cognitive, emotional, and/or behavioral nature.
      d. (Assists, Counsels) students regarding (career, educational, social, emotional) decisions.
      e. Constructs and maintains comprehensive case studies.
      f. Collaborates with other staff in the development of the school policy handbook by contributing information in area of expertise.
      g. Conducts orientation sessions for (incoming, newly trans-ferred) students and/or their parents in all areas regarding assimilation into the school.
      h. Visits sending schools and conducts informational sessions for prospective students.
      i. Coordinates the school (achievement testing program, Career Day, field trip, etc.) program.
      j. Serves on relevant (school, district) committees in area of expertise.

   B. Level of Expertise
      a. Adheres to all required (ethical, professional) practices in the performance of duties.
      b. Collects, interprets, and applies information gathered about students to strategies geared to promote students' best interests.
      c. (Interprets, Describes, Explains) (district, school) written pol-icy regarding area of expertise to (faculty, parents, community groups, etc.).
      d. Compiles and utilizes list of (agencies, programs, profession-als) who provide (student, family) services.
      e. Knowledgeable of all phases of student development as they relate to students' cognitive, social, and emotional growth.
      f. Able to (interpret, analyze, explain) achievement test (results, format, norms, etc.).

g. Makes appropriate use of (referrals, resources) to aid students.
h. In consistent compliance with the Family Education Rights and Privacy Act in the collection of student information.
i. Utilizes a variety of techniques to assess, analyze, and monitor students' (academic progress, career goals, development, etc.).
j. Periodically reviews and assesses records in order to confirm their accuracy.

C. Preparation and Organization
   a. Maintains and distributes all forms and directives required to complete student referrals.
   b. Maintains current listings of (colleges, universities, vocational/technical schools, secondary schools, etc.) and makes them available to staff, students, and parents.
   c. Maintains a listing of contact persons connected with (business, educational, social service, medical) institutions.
   d. Keeps current with reports related to areas of involvement.
   e. Promptly receives and returns calls and other forms of communication.
   f. Transmits records of (graduating, transferring) students to receiving schools.
   g. Reviews the records of students transferring in or out for accuracy.
   h. Maintains a running record of specific students' attendance, and confers with (classroom teacher, student attendance counselor, parents) (when, where) improvement is indicated.
   i. Incorporates flexibility in schedule to allow time to provide (emergency, impromptu, personalized, etc.) service where needed.
   j. Compiles informational literature relating to career or employment choices and makes this available for use by students and their parents.

D. Related Duties
   a. Collaborates with the (Child Study Team, classroom teacher) during the sequential steps of the referral process.
   b. (Researches, Visits) (secondary schools, institutions of higher learning) in order to become conversant with their (program, financial aid, etc.) opportunities.
   c. (Examines, Observes) (characteristics, needs) of referred students and (confers with, assists) (staff, parents, students) to develop strategies to improve their school performance.
   d. Provides relevant information regarding student progress to (professionals, agencies, etc.) in order to obtain needed services for students and their families.
   e. (Participates in, Conducts) conferences regarding students' (behavioral, academic, interpersonal) needs.

     f. Coordinates school's (schedule of guidance services, Career Day activities, assessment program, graduation class activities, etc.).

     g. Assists students who exhibit specific talents in finding opportunities for advanced (training, classes).

     h. Accompanies (small groups, classes, individuals, students and parents) on field trips to (specify off-site trip, e.g., college interviews).

     i. Assists students and parents to plan a meaningful program of studies, including (electives, sports activities, the arts, etc.).

     j. Provides (whole-class, small-group) in-class counseling sessions in the area of (personal, interpersonal) growth.

E. Interpersonal Domain

     a. Assists students in the development of skills that promote school and personal (growth, success).

     b. Allows students to (relate, share, explain) their concerns and provides helpful (assistance, suggestions).

     c. Helps parents to (interpret, understand) (assessment data, test scores, progress reports) and their relationship to their child's progress.

     d. Assists and supports students and their parents as they make (educational, vocational, career, occupational) decisions.

     e. Makes himself or herself available to (staff, students, parents) on a continuing basis.

     f. (Readily, Consistently, Willingly) responds to requests and other stated needs from staff, students, and/or parents.

     g. Makes himself or herself available to (staff, students, parents) (during, before, after) the school day, and other designated times.

     h. Respects the (concerns, beliefs, customs, culture) of students and parents in the performance of duties.

     i. Maintains an environment that is conducive to students' need for (privacy, validation, candid dialogue, calm, acceptance).

     j. Collects, interprets, and utilizes data gathered on the progress of graduates to support needed (adaptations, enhancements, adjustments) to the guidance program.

School Attendance Counselor

A. Specific Tasks

     a. (Collects, Collates, Researches) data in preparation for (legal, court) action.

     b. Works with (law enforcement, social service, juvenile justice, court) and related agencies in order to (track, remediate) truants.

     c. Follows through on all referrals made by the school relevant to student (absenteeism, truancy, lateness).

    d. Communicates relationship of regular school attendance to academic achievement to (students, parents).

    e. Prepares cogent, accurate, and informative findings, conclusions, and recommendations.

    f. Conducts (exhaustive, detailed, thorough) investigations into students' record of (absences, lateness, truancy).

    g. Makes regular visits to schools and carries out assigned duties.

    h. Demonstrates comprehensive knowledge of (district, state, school) policies as they relate to student attendance.

    i. Prepares social case histories.

    j. Develops and implements the (appropriate, effective, required) course of action based on individual circumstances surrounding each student.

B. Level of Expertise

    a. Is (knowledgeable of, adept at) the use of (electronic, computerized, manual) (equipment, techniques) associated with the performance of duties.

    b. Is (knowledgeable of, adept at) the use of a range of software programs specific to the recording of attendance data.

    c. Able to (read, interpret, convey) district or state rules and regulations relative to school attendance.

    d. Collaborates with staff to formulate strategies geared to create or adjust (practices, programs, techniques) presently used to decrease truancy.

    e. Possesses an in-depth knowledge of (school and state law, court procedures) as they pertain to student attendance.

    f. Utilizes effective (questioning, investigation techniques) to reveal cases of (illegal residency, truancy, delinquency, neglect).

    g. (Initiates, Creates, Plans) effective (prevention, intervention) strategies.

    h. Proactive in identifying attendance patterns that indicate conditions of (abuse, neglect, truancy, etc.).

    i. Advises (classroom teachers, Child Study Team, social service agencies, juvenile justice agencies) seeking resolutions to situations that impede students' progress.

    j. Develops and implements the (appropriate, effective, required) course of action based on individual circumstances surrounding each student.

C. Preparation and Organization

    a. Possesses all academic and/or other certification required by (district, state) mandate.

    b. Prepares data in a manner that can be readily interpreted and utilized to determine attendance patterns.

    c. Maintains accurate records of student (census, absenteeism, attendance, transfers).

      d. Manages multi-school assignments, providing services equally and consistently.

      e. Utilizes computer technology to maintain records.

      f. Maintains accurate (records, data, files)

      g. Is thoroughly familiar with the geographic layout of the assigned area.

      h. Maintains an excellent record of personal attendance.

      i. Shares case (data, files) with school counselors.

      j. Maintains listing of affordable student and family services, including private (testing, counseling) services.

D. Related Duties

      a. Collaborates with (school, district, community, social service, charitable, volunteer, religious, etc.) organizations and agencies to gain needed services for students and their families.

      b. Represents (school, district) during court appearances.

      c. Cooperates with (public, private) welfare agencies.

      d. (Willingly, Effectively, Conscientiously) performs all (delegated, assigned) non-instructional duties.

      e. Works with school authorities to assure educational opportunities for students returning to regular school attendance.

      f. (Follows up, Enforces) remedial action determined by the (school authorities, district, courts).

      g. Speaks with community and business groups in order to communicate the school's "stay in school" initiatives and to solicit support for the program.

      h. Makes home visitations during nonschool hours, where feasible.

      i. Works with staff to find (programs, activities) that motivate students to (come to, stay in) school.

      j. Recommends alternative school placement, where needed.

E. Interpersonal Domain

      a. Works to (assist, refer, counsel) families on matters that impact negatively on student attendance.

      b. Cooperates with all school personnel that impact school attendance.

      c. Is (familiar with, respectful of) (familial, religious, ethnic, etc.) (customs, mores, opinions) of the community.

      d. Works with parents or guardians to determine the cause of student (absences, lateness).

      e. (Meets, Cooperates, Collaborates) with (parent, teacher, community) groups to formulate strategies for increasing student attendance.

      f. (Communicates, Stresses) the relationship of attendance to academic (growth, success, progress) to (students, parents).

      g. (Aids, Helps) parents or guardians to accept accountability for students' regular school attendance.

    h. Communicates with parents or guardians regarding students' attendance via (telephone, e-mail, notes, letters, home visits).

    i. Becomes familiar with neighborhood (business owners, residents, law enforcement, etc.).

    j. Establishes a nonpunitive relationship with students and their parents.

Student Assistance Counselor

A. Specific Tasks

    a. Possesses all of the prerequisite academic background and certification required for the position.

    b. Demonstrates knowledge of student (norms, disabilities, characteristics, approaches to learning, test scores, etc.).

    c. Provides counseling on both an individual and group basis.

    d. Maintains comprehensive records of students' progress and performance in the regular classroom setting and other areas in which instruction is given.

    e. (Attends, Participates in, Engages in) professional (seminars, workshops, conferences) in order to keep current in area of expertise.

    f. Collaborates with all professionals in an attempt to positively (engage, reinstate, direct, redirect) student into a stable position in the class or school.

    g. (Assists, Counsels) students to make appropriate choices when considering (remaining in, leaving) school.

    h. Conferences with (classroom teacher, parents) regarding the collection of (evidence, documentation, anecdotal records) that support developing a referral on the student.

    i. Engages students in guidance (sessions, activities) as appropriate.

    j. Conducts (evaluative, follow-up) procedures to determine progress made by all students on his or her roster.

B. Level of Expertise

    a. Expedites student records in a confidential and professional manner.

    b. Articulates (school, district) informational programs in order to assist students and their families.

    c. Reads (journals, texts, periodicals, reports, etc.) related to (innovative, current, new) strategies geared toward the delivery of services.

    d. Designs (strategies, techniques) for students to employ in coping with (daily living, school life, personal life, peer pressure, family problems, substance abuse).

    e. Reacts appropriately and effectively on matters related to students' (well-being, growth, progress).

    f. Maintains a collection of reference materials to aid students when making (educational, vocational, life, employment) choices.

    g. (Interprets, Communicates, Reviews, Analyzes) assessment data in order to direct students toward (measures, resources, techniques) leading to improved results.

    h. Adheres to ethical practices in the performance of duties.

    i. Collaborates effectively with (professional, community, social service) agencies in an effort to prevent students' premature exit from (school, formal education, home).

    j. Functions productively with guidance colleagues and larger school community.

C. Preparation and Organization

    a. Develops and maintains professionally prepared documents.

    b. Utilizes software specific to tasks related to the position.

    c. Collaborates with all personnel relating to students' (attendance, academic, behavioral and emotional states of being).

    d. Shares data with all relevant personnel.

    e. Demonstrates professional (speaking, writing, counseling) skills.

    f. Maintains an environment in which students feel (validated, safe, comfortable).

    g. Shares reports concerning students' (progress, ability, needs) with authorized personnel.

    h. Maintains current listings of all (agencies, schools, medical facilities, etc.) that partner with the school system in the delivery of services to disaffected students.

    i. (Answers, Responds to) (inquiries, communication, referrals, requests) promptly and effectively.

    j. Is thoroughly familiar with the genesis, present status, and projected resolution of each student's case.

D. Related Duties

    a. Forges a relationship with outside (agencies, corporations, educational institutions, philanthropists, etc.) willing to assist students in realizing their goals and aspirations.

    b. Serves as a source of informational data for professionals regarding issues relating to students' (disciplinary, personal, juvenile justice, family court) (background, experiences).

    c. Students' (employment, housing, financial, continuing education) needs are addressed in the course of providing needed services.

    d. Maintains communication with classroom teachers relating to students' classroom (academic, behavioral, attendance) record.

    e. Engages students in (self-help, self-assessment, self-actualizing) exercises.

      f. Assists students in making (career, employment, life) choices.

      g. (Reviews, Investigates, Evaluates) incidents of students' (suspension, expulsion).

      h. Confers with students and parents upon students' reentry into school after suspension.

      i. Facilitates students' transfers to (alternative, vocational, residential, rehabilitation) facilities.

      j. Makes court appearances and supplies requested documentation for (juvenile justice, family court) matters.

E. Interpersonal Domain

      a. Provides feedback to (students, parents) relative to (educational choices, graduation, placement, employment options, etc.).

      b. Serves as a (mentor, advocate, confidant) when interacting with students.

      c. Works with parents or guardian to find needed (afterschool activities, child care, counseling) to provide for students' (safety, remedial services, etc.) after the regular school day.

      d. Establishes a caring, productive, and professional relationship with students and their families.

      e. (Develops strategies, Takes steps) to assist students in building a positive (feeling, attitude) of (self-worth, "I can," being part of the group, worthiness, etc.).

      f. Helps students find ways to (navigate, overcome, avoid, minimize, cope with) obstacles.

      g. Helps students to (identify, maximize) their (talents, skills, assets, opportunities, abilities).

      h. (Empathizes, Sympathizes) with students, where indicated.

      i. Serves as an available resource for (students, parents, colleagues) in area of expertise.

      j. (Possesses, Projects) a (calm, nurturing, no-nonsense) demeanor.

Suggested "Pats on the Back"

This section is geared to provide you with ideas for choosing just the right words to applaud exemplary performance. We hope you will have cause to make liberal use of these "pats on the back."

1. You are a valuable member of our team of counselors. Your contribution as (name type of counselor) to our efforts to provide student services is noted—and appreciated.

2. Our staff can rely on you to quickly and efficiently follow through on their (referrals, concerns) and work diligently through to completion on each case.

3. You demonstrate your level of (concern, interest) in the students by the manner in which you provide follow-up (assistance, counseling) to ensure successful resolution to their situation.

4. Because of your efforts, our students have shown greater (motivation to, interest in) adopting (sound attendance, remaining in school, taking interest in school, their studies, etc.).

5. You have been identified by our (students, parents) as a counselor who cares. There is no greater accolade!

6. Thank you for going beyond what was required in your attempts to help the students. You exemplify the adage, "never give up."

7. Your data collection on each (case, referral, student) is comprehensive, accurate, and gives evidence of your attention to detail.

8. A hallmark of your counseling has been the manner in which you encourage students to reach beyond expected limits. Thank you for helping them expand their (dreams, horizons, options).

9. It is clear that you have the students' welfare as your primary objective. You give each student individualized attention and the support he or she seeks and needs.

10. You provide your students with the (self-esteem, support, motivation, lifeline, etc.) that they need to (make sound life choices, stay in school, set goals, strive to do better, overcome obstacles, etc.). Thank you for your efforts.

Section IV

DISCIPLINARIANS

Crisis Intervention Advisor, Dean, In-School Suspension Staff

This section assists the administrator in determining if basic qualifications, expertise, and requirements for successful fulfillment of duties inherent to the job title have been demonstrated.

Performance Statements

Note: With occasional editing, Performance Statements are interchangeable between job titles in this section, when appropriate.

Crisis Intervention Advisor, Dean

A. Specific Tasks
   a. (Coordinates, Mentors) efforts of all professional personnel involved in student discipline and related factors.
   b. Accepts and utilizes input from all reliable sources when developing individualized discipline plans for students.
   c. Works closely with support personnel, including paraprofessionals, school security, and other staff in the implementation of the school Code of Conduct.
   d. Collaborates with home instruction teachers and classroom teachers concerning students' academic progress.
   e. Attends and participates in district meetings as they relate to students' (suspension, expulsion) procedures.
   f. Employs appropriate methods and materials to meet (stated, program) objectives.
   g. Consults with school and community support personnel, including (student assistance, guidance, attendance counselors, Child Study Team, school nurse) regarding students' progress.
   h. (Enforces, Implements, Upholds) (school rules, administrative regulations, Board of Education policy, Code of Conduct, standard operating procedures) in carrying out duties.

       i. Completes and submits accurate, comprehensive, and timely reports.

       j. Exacts due process and upholds students' rights in the performance of duty.

B. Level of Expertise

     a. Contributes to the construction of school disciplinary regulations.

     b. Conversant with current hardware and software related to area of expertise.

     c. Assists classroom teachers with the development of effective behavior modification strategies.

     d. Formulates individualized program of (rehabilitation, behavior modification) for students in need of same.

     e. Familiar with (respected, current) theories and practices in area of expertise.

     f. Provides services to classified and regular education students.

     g. Possesses the ability to defuse (crisis, volatile) situations.

     h. (Contributes to, Participates in) district efforts to decrease incidences of negative behavior among the student population.

     i. (Aware of, Familiar with) (substance abuse, gang affiliations, incidences of abuse and neglect) within the student population.

     j. (Knowledgeable of, Understands) the characteristics of (child, adolescent, teen) growth and development, and related behaviors.

C. Preparation and Organization

     a. Manages a calendar of (appointments, mentoring, mediations, consultations, evaluative procedures) related to follow-up on students' progress.

     b. Participates in schoolwide initiatives in order to (develop, maintain) a learning environment free from disruption.

     c. Maintains an environment that is calming and protected from needless stimuli.

     d. Maintains accurate, comprehensive records.

     e. Takes measures to improve professional (competencies, productivity).

     f. Develops and implements a variety of preventive and/or intervention strategies.

     g. Makes timely responses to (requests, inquiries, etc.).

     h. Documents all (conferences, meetings, incidents, consultations, infractions, etc.).

     i. Demonstrates sound mediation (abilities, strategies, crisis intervention skills).

     j. Develops and maintains a current listing of facilities and services for students in need of (alternative, home instruction, juvenile justice) academic programs.

D. Related Duties
  a. Participates in (meetings, conferences, workshops) related to area of expertise.
  b. Assists in the development of policies and procedures, as well as the ongoing operation of school's in-school suspension program.
  c. Makes all required (court, agency, etc.) visitations relating to behavioral aspects of disaffected students.
  d. (Collaborates, Confers) with counselor regarding student's program of behavior modification.
  e. Consults with medical or health personnel relative to (physical, emotional, psychological) genesis of student behavior.
  f. Seeks (input from, assistance of) the Child Study Team in formulating (strategies, programs) for students demonstrating acting-out behaviors.
  g. Seeks innovative methods of involving students in (positive, self-actualizing) behaviors.
  h. Exposes students to positive role models from the (arts, sports world, community, business world, etc.).
  i. Participates in (district, schoolwide) (stay-in-school, school pride, etc.) initiatives and activities.
  j. Serves under the direction of the school administration in the performance of duties.

E. Interpersonal Domain
  a. Communicates with (parents or guardians, staff, classroom teachers, agencies) in a timely manner.
  b. Involves students in (self-assessment, counseling, behavior and anger management) activities.
  c. Encourages students to become involved in school activities in an effort to (alleviate, eliminate) their sense of alienation from involvement in the mainstream of school life.
  d. Lends assistance to school's effort to maintain a positive, safe, and orderly environment.
  e. Welcomes parental interaction and remains available to assist in the role of (advisor, mediator, friend).
  f. Establishes a climate of mutual respect between self and students.
  g. (Implements, Upholds) behavior modification strategies in a (nonpunitive, nonconfrontational) manner.
  h. Projects and maintains a positive, supportive, and caring demeanor.
  i. Encourages and assists students to get in touch with the (positive, productive) side of their nature.
  j. Available to assist students after their reentry into (school, the regular classroom, mainstream school attendance).

In-School Suspension Staff

A. Specific Tasks
   a. Demonstrates knowledge of (guidelines, rules and regulations, standard operating procedures) of the In-School Suspension program.
   b. Possesses effective (intervention, mediation, counseling) skills.
   c. Adheres to the (highest, expected) professional and ethical standards.
   d. Implements the (academic, behavioral, remedial) program formulated for students in the In-School Suspension program by the (classroom teacher, Student Assistance Counselor, administration, etc.) for students serving in-school suspension.
   e. Reads referrals and implements suggested strategies geared to promote positive student behavior.
   f. Maintains accurate and comprehensive records on each student assigned to the program.
   g. Develops and employs a variety of effective behavior modification (strategies, techniques).
   h. Provides ongoing reports to (administrators, supervisor, teacher, parents) based on (findings, information) gathered relative to each student's suspension status.
   i. Develops lesson plans designed to provide practical learning and/or behavior modification experiences for assigned students.
   j. Keeps students productively engaged during time served in the In-school Suspension program.

B. Level of Expertise
   a. Demonstrates knowledge of (child, adolescent, teenage) growth and development and related behavioral norms of the age group.
   b. Knowledgeable of curriculum content of all grade levels and provides a continuum program of academics for students serving periods of in-school suspension.
   c. Anticipates, defuses, and resolves (stressful, volatile, acting-out) situations.
   d. Communicates the design and methodology of the In-School Suspension program to students, parents, and other interested parties.
   e. Collaborates with students, parents, and teachers in developing behavior and academic contracts.
   f. (Follows up, Evaluates) the progress of students readmitted to the general school population.
   g. Utilizes the services of paraprofessionals in an appropriate and productive manner.

h. Formulates and implements a program of conflict resolution and sound interpersonal social interaction for students.
i. Maintains the integrity of the program and the confidentiality of the assigned students.
j. Evaluates program referrals and related documents for completeness and accuracy.

C. Preparation and Organization
   a. Maintains comprehensive records of student (referrals, attendance, behavior, progress).
   b. Maintains individual student folders.
   c. Maintains a firm and caring demeanor.
   d. Maintains all materials necessary to provide full academic services to students assigned to the program.
   e. Requires students to make constructive use of time while assigned to the program.
   f. Models and expects students to uphold sound personal habits, decorum, and dress.
   g. Consistently upholds and enforces the school and district Code of Conduct.
   h. Develops and adheres to individual students' schedule of services, including counseling, etc.
   i. Maintains anecdotal records and other related records.
   j. Maintains list of available referral forms required to (request, recommend, obtain) services for students.

D. Related Duties
   a. Conducts (workshops, discussions) for professional staff during which program activities and behavior modification strategies are outlined.
   b. Closely monitors the (attendance, activities, behavior) of students assigned to the In-School Suspension program.
   c. Willing to (eat lunch with a student, arrive before class, stay after school) to demonstrate (concern for, interest in) students' concerns and need for (extra time, individualized attention).
   d. Provides services for students serving short-term as well as long-term assignments in the In-School Suspension program.
   e. Works closely with assigned security and/or professional police staff.
   f. Demonstrates knowledge of the dynamics of negative street culture on student behavior and seeks solutions to remove those influences.
   g. Seeks partnership with (community, religious, social service) groups to initiate (programs, opportunities) to support student goals to (remain in school, adopt productive behaviors, change negative attitudes, gain feeling of self-worth).

      h. Participates in post-suspension conferences with students, administrators, teachers, and parents.

      i. Contributes to the referral procedure for pre-classification of students, in area of knowledge of student and level of expertise.

      j. (Works with, Assists) (counselors, teachers) in the development of (prevention, intervention, remedial) plans and contracts for students.

  E. Interpersonal Domain

      a. Consults with parents and all relevant professional staff concerning a variety of academic and behavioral factors regarding students assigned to in-school suspension.

      b. Helps students to develop sound (coping, self-reflective, impulse-control, behavioral, interpersonal) skills and abilities.

      c. Maintains a learning environment in which students receive and give respect.

      d. Treats referred student as an individual and provides services geared toward each student's needs.

      e. Provides a forum in which students feel free to (articulate, participate, share concerns and fears, etc.) and to respect those freedoms in others.

      f. (Articulates, Brings, Communicates) the message of the goals and objectives of the In-School Suspension program to (parents, parent groups, community).

      g. Assists families in crisis with needed referrals to professionals, agencies, and support groups.

      h. Provides a forum for students to discuss (grievances, rationale for choices made, problems, concerns, etc.) and suggested (remedies, solutions) for those issues.

      i. Maintains a climate in which cultural and ethnic diversity is validated and respected.

      j. Interacts (willingly, easily, cooperatively, productively) with (students, parents, staff).

Suggested "Pats on the Back"

This section is geared to provide you with ideas for choosing just the right words to applaud exemplary performance. We hope you will have cause to make liberal use of these "pats on the back."

1. Our teachers feel that their (concerns, requests) are validated by the (timely, productive) manner in which you follow through on their referrals. Thank you for your efforts.

2. You consistently uphold and reinforce our (Student Code of Conduct, standard operating procedure) in a nonpunitive way. Our students benefit from this structure.

3. Thank you for providing quality instruction to our students while they are assigned out of their regular classroom. Our teachers recognize your efforts.

4. We recognize the challenges that (you face, are presented) in working with the (disaffected, challenged) (child, student). Your (counseling, support) provides incentives for these students to work toward rejoining the (mainstream population, regular classroom).

5. Your manner is powerful and effective, yet never punitive.

6. You have been instrumental in resolving (issues, problems) that might have reached an impasse without your efforts. Thank you.

7. You communicate with students and their parents in a manner that makes them a part of the solution and partners in our effort to provide a safe and positive climate for learning.

8. You help each student to realize that he or she can aim for the future and to achieve by using the skills that he or she possesses.

9. You provided a valuable service in devoting your time and expertise during (specify the activity or incident). Your efforts helped all of us to pull through a (stressful, challenging) (time, event).

10. Students come away from your office equipped with renewed vision and reinforced coping skills. Thank you for supporting and encouraging them.

Section V

HEALTH AND MEDICAL PERSONNEL

Health Care Advisor, School Nurse, School Psychologist

This section assists the administrator in determining if basic qualifications, expertise, and requirements for successful fulfillment of duties inherent to the job title have been demonstrated.

Performance Statements

Note: With occasional editing, Performance Statements are interchangeable between job titles in this section, when appropriate.

Health Care Advisor

A. Specific Tasks
    a. Provides health instruction based on a sequential, prescribed course of study.
    b. Provides scheduled health instruction to individuals, small groups, and whole-class groups.
    c. Collaborates with other health care professionals and classroom teacher to construct, recommend, and execute the health curriculum.
    d. Develops lesson objectives aligned with the health curriculum.
    e. Conforms to all (rules, regulations, codes, guidelines, restrictions, etc.) in the performance of duty.
    f. Utilizes district-approved (curriculum, literature, materials).
    g. Formulates (reports, student records, etc.) that are current, comprehensive, and accurate.
    h. (Coordinates, Develops, Monitors) school health education initiatives.
    i. Serves as a resource person in the field of health care for (faculty, students, parents).
    j. (Evaluates, Measures) health program (outcomes, effectiveness) through a variety of measures that are aligned with the instructional objectives of the program.

B. Level of Expertise
   a. Coordinates health education with other fields of study, using a cross-content (approach, method) of providing instruction.
   b. Well versed on new developments and research in the field.
   c. (Demonstrates knowledge of, Is adept in the use of) computer technology and software specific to the health program.
   d. Develops an instructional program based on the appropriate diagnosis of students' (developmental, learning) characteristics.
   e. Maintains memberships and actively participates in professional organizations.
   f. Has (training, completed courses, gained experience) in the (biological, physical, behavioral, health care) sciences.
   g. Committed to an ongoing program of continuing professional development.
   h. Provides students with information regarding career opportunities in health occupations and their required entry-level skills.
   i. Utilizes computer technology to provide health education (programs, information, developments, research) to (students, faculty).
   j. Uses, and teaches students to use, correct terminology when defining, explaining, and discussing health (matters, concerns).

C. Preparation and Organization
   a. (Maintains, Makes available) a range of health-related materials for use by students and/or faculty.
   b. Maintains a professional library.
   c. Maintains memberships in professional organizations.
   d. (Prepares, Utilizes) (resource units, study guides, related support materials) as a basis for planning and implementing lessons.
   e. Develops (hands-on displays, visuals, models) of health-related learning aids in the form of (describe types of displays).
   f. Maintains a lending resource facility that is accessible and has a functional use for teachers and other professional staff.
   g. Maintains a professional library of current publications and periodicals for students and/or faculty.
   h. Prepares invoices and related records of supplies and equipment.
   i. (Collaborates, Works) with the administration to assure that adequate funding, staffing, and facilities are allotted to the health care program.
   j. Strives to ensure that instructional materials are adequate to fulfill program needs.

D. Related Duties
   a. Participates in the preparation of courses of study, and the selection of textbooks, reference materials, and other instructional aids.
   b. Conducts health education in-service instruction for (faculty, parents, community).

   c. Serves as a liaison to facilitate visitations by health care
      professionals to the classroom.
   d. Collaborates with classroom teachers regarding the integration
      of health care instruction into the regular program of study.
   e. As a result of his or her health care courses, students gain knowl-
      edge of local, state, national, and world health-related issues.
   f. Teaches students to (monitor, gain an awareness of, evaluate)
      the status of their own health.
   g. Works with administration, parents, and other health care
      professionals to (detect, give treatment referrals for, monitor)
      instances of students' substance abuse.
   h. Effectively collects, analyzes, and interprets student health
      care data.
   i. Develops and implements an ad hoc committee of health care
      professionals and faculty members willing to advise and
      deliver services geared to meet student needs.
   j. Seeks (funding, partnerships, grants) to gain additional ser-
      vices for students and their families.

E. Interpersonal Domain
   a. Helps students adopt and retain healthy (living patterns,
      choices, behaviors).
   b. Works productively with other health care professionals as
      well as the general faculty.
   c. Maintains an environment in which student health (con-
      cerns, needs) are validated and assistance is given, where
      indicated.
   d. Health care facility is functional, safe, aesthetically pleasing,
      and well maintained.
   e. Consistently (available, accessible) to (students, parents, staff).
   f. Assists physicians and health care staff when administering
      mandated health-related tests.
   g. Volunteers services for (school-, community-) based activi-
      ties, including health fairs, mobile health-screening units, etc.
   h. Collaborates with community resource health care providers
      to obtain follow-up care for students and/or their families.
   i. Provides opportunities for students to gain an awareness of
      dangerous practices that have negative impact on health.
   j. Promotes health care program by means of (describe public
      relations activity).

School Nurse

A. Specific Tasks
   a. Assists physicians in conducting medical or physical exami-
      nations of students.
   b. Administers first aid in cases of accident and/or illness.

    c. Administers prescribed dosages of prescription medicines.

    d. Seeks emergency medical attention for students or faculty, when needed.

    e. Administers all district- (authorized, approved) medical tests and examinations, including (Mantoux, vision, hearing, height, weight, etc.).

    f. Authorizes exclusion of staff and students from school due to suspected communicable and other illnesses.

    g. Assists physician in administering vaccinations and other inoculations.

    h. Maintains accurate, comprehensive, and timely (health, building and lavatory inspections, supply, etc.) records.

    i. Prepares and submits all required reports as mandated by the (name state).

    j. Notifies administration of condition that impact negatively on the health, safety, and welfare of students and staff.

B. Level of Expertise

    a. Conducts (discussions, demonstrations, health talks, etc.) and instruction on subject of (personal hygiene, diet, sanitation, substance abuse, etc.).

    b. Demonstrates (knowledge of, ability to perform) all of the duties inherent in the position.

    c. Demonstrates knowledge of, and follows, all district medical policies and procedures.

    d. Demonstrates the ability to utilize various types of technological, electronic, and/or manual recording and information systems.

    e. Compiles clear, sound, accurate, and informative reports containing (findings, conclusions, recommendations).

    f. Reviews the (inoculation, vaccination, health records) of all students entering school for the first time or transferred in from out-of-district locations.

    g. Maximizes the use of technology in order to (bring, keep) records current.

    h. Demonstrates effective (writing, speaking, nursing) skills.

    i. Maintains record of (health, psychological, medical, therapeutic) services available to classified and typically functioning student population.

    j. Administers prescribed treatment and ensures that prescribed measures are carried out for the correction of special defects.

C. Preparation and Organization

    a. Maintains appearance consistent with the appropriate attire of a health care professional.

    b. Maintains records of health services prescribed for classified students, as outlined in their IEPs.

    c. Schedules program of student health-screening activities, according to district or state mandate.

    d. Maintains records, files in a highly professional manner.

    e. Obtains, stores, inventories, safeguards, and makes proper use of medical equipment and supplies.

    f. Maintains a medical and health reference library.

    g. Analyzes, organizes, and paces workload in order to complete all assigned duties in a timely manner.

    h. Maintains a directory of (student body, personnel) data, including (contact persons, physician, special health concerns, medication, etc.).

    i. Secures all medicines and/or medical devices in a safe and secure manner.

    j. Remains current with technological materials and practices used in the field.

D. Related Duties

    a. Inspects classrooms, lavatories, and other school areas in order to ensure that they are maintained in a clean and sanitary condition.

    b. (Makes, Provides) appropriate medical referrals for (students, families, school personnel).

    c. Conducts (lectures, demonstrations) for students regarding general health and hygienic practices.

    d. Interviews parents in order to obtain needed information regarding students' previous or existing health (conditions, concerns).

    e. Examines and implements physicians' (orders, notes, recommendations) for students and faculty returning to regular school attendance after period of medical (release, absence).

    f. Seeks (agencies, philanthropists, charities, volunteers, individuals, etc.) willing to assist student and/or families to acquire health aids, including (eyeglasses, hearing aids, etc.).

    g. Reports all incidences of communicable disease to administrators, parents, and appropriate agencies.

    h. Collaborates closely with (child-protective, related health, public health, juvenile justice, family counseling) agencies.

    i. Serves on (name committee) and related professional affiliations.

    j. Attends and renders health care services at school (sports, off-site, recreational) events.

E. Interpersonal Domain

    a. Maintains calm demeanor when providing (emergency, routine, crisis) health care to staff or students.

    b. Maintains an environment conducive to privacy, confidentiality, and efficient health care.

    c. Maintains an aesthetically pleasing health facility in which the atmosphere is calm and comforting.

    d. Works harmoniously with (associates, social service agencies, parent organizations, community groups, agencies, etc.) in area of health-related issues.

    e. Assists parents and families to acquire needed health services from school and/or outside agencies, organizations.

    f. Conducts (workshops, demonstrations) for parent and/or community groups on topics related to students' sound health habits, including (nutrition, exercise, substance abuse prevention, abuse and neglect, etc.).

    g. Communicates with parents or guardians regarding all health issues concerning their children.

    h. Possesses knowledge of (cultural, ethnic, diverse) (practices, restrictions, concerns) as they pertain to providing health care services to students.

    i. Conducts holistic assessments and practices when providing services to students.

    j. (Assists, Treats) students who experience (illness, injury, distress) until the arrival of (parents, guardian, ambulance) or other appropriate medical emergency personnel.

School Psychologist

A. Specific Tasks

    a. Makes diagnosis of special learning disabilities, in terms of students' (mental, physical, environmental, psychological) status, after performing appropriate tests.

    b. In collaboration with members of the Child Study Team (CST), administers psychological evaluations of students' cognitive, social, adaptive, and emotional (abilities, disabilities).

    c. Develops psychological evaluations as a member of the Child Study Team and related agencies.

    d. Collaborates with and makes recommendations to (administrators, nurses, speech or occupational therapist, guidance counselor, classroom teacher, etc.) in regard to required services for classified students.

    e. Plans and develops Individual Educational Plan (IEP) for students.

    f. Serves as an integral part of all (meetings, conferences) relating to students with disabilities, from initial referral, through to appropriate placement, and beyond.

    g. Works with members of the CST to expedite the referral process in a professional and timely manner.

    h. Serves as a member of the School Student Referral Review Committee.

    i. (Assumes, Assigns, Delineates) (case, team) management responsibilities for the Child Study Team.

    j. Organizes and defines criteria to measure the prescribed educational program for classified students.

B. Level of Expertise

    a. In collaboration with CST members, contributes expertise in the selection of (literature, manipulatives, supplies, equipment, etc.) to be used in the delivery of services to students with disabilities.

    b. Competent in the use of various electronic and/or manual recording and information systems.

    c. Competent in the use of software specific to the field of expertise.

    d. Knowledgeable of policies and procedures mandated by the district or state in the performance of duties.

    e. In conjunction with members of the CST, administers psychological evaluations to determine students' (cognitive, social, adaptive, emotional) abilities.

    f. Utilizes appropriate techniques, procedures, and language when (reporting, documenting) assessment data.

    g. (Knowledgeable of, Abides by) federal, state, and district laws, rules, and regulations as they pertain to the diagnosis and recommendation for delivery of services to students with disabilities.

    h. Shares accountability for the accurate diagnosis and (suitability, viability) of recommended services for students with disabilities.

    i. Provides (services, recommendations) in (specialized education schools, residential facilities, homebound environment, hospitals) for students with disabilities.

    j. In collaboration with the Learning Disabilities Specialist, (recommends, suggests) (specialized, adaptive) teaching techniques for use by (classroom and inclusion teachers) working with students with disabilities.

C. Preparation and Organization

    a. Maintains highly professional and comprehensive records.

    b. Develops and delivers all records (requested, mandated, required) by the district or state.

    c. Maintains listings of available (out-of-district, residential, etc.) facilities that (accommodate, provide needed services to) students with disabilities.

    d. Obtains and upholds all laws, rules, and regulations governing special education in the performance of duties.

    e. Maintains a neat, aesthetic, and professional workspace.

    f. Adheres to time (frame, parameters) for completing psychological (evaluation, workup) on all applicants.

g. Utilizes technology, where appropriate, in order to enhance productivity in the performance of duties.

h. Knowledgeable of the general education curriculum, and assists in making needed modifications to meet the academic needs of students with disabilities.

i. Reviews all reports for (comprehensiveness, omissions, errors, timeliness, signatures, etc.).

j. Remains current with all revisions to laws, rules, regulations, policies, and procedures governing students with disabilities.

D. Related Duties

a. Represents the district or school at (state, national) conferences in area of expertise.

b. (Organizes, Conducts, Participates in) in-service (workshops, seminars) for (teachers, parents) concerning a variety of issues relevant to the diagnosis, treatment, placement, and care of students with disabilities.

c. Conducts (individual, group) therapy sessions.

d. Observes, assesses, and makes recommendations regarding the classroom learning (environment, conditions) relative to the progress of students with disabilities.

e. Communicates with (local, state) parent groups concerning policies and procedures relating to the delivery of services to students with disabilities.

f. Makes recommendations to school or district administrators concerning the degree to which the needs of students with disabilities are being met.

g. Participates in the interview process for candidates for employment in special education program.

h. Drafts all required correspondence in the course of the performance of duties.

i. Assists teachers of the handicapped to formulate (behavior modification, life skills, interpersonal relationship) techniques for their classes.

j. Conducts classroom observations to (determine, assess) suitability of (placement, program of instruction) for students with disabilities.

E. Interpersonal Domain

a. Provides (expertise, assistance) to classroom teachers in matters of student behavior modification (techniques, strategies).

b. Assists (classroom teachers) to look beyond students' disability in order to enhance opportunities for students with disabilities.

c. Shares all findings with Child Study Team and appropriate staff members.

   d. Attends (courses, seminars, workshops, conferences) related
      to the field of expertise in order to remain current.
   e. (Sensitive to, Aware of) (cultural, ethnic) (issues, beliefs, con-
      cerns) of students with disabilities and their families relative
      to (diagnosis, placement, services, etc.).
   f. Actively engages with parents in all (meetings, conferences)
      pertaining to students' (referral, diagnosis, placement,
      progress).
   g. (Enjoys, Maintains) a (collegial, professional, productive)
      relationship with (CST members, staff, parents, students).
   h. Consults with CST members to provide skillful, timely, and
      productive services.
   i. (Collaborates, Communicates) with (social service, juvenile
      justice, community, etc.) groups and/or agencies in order to
      gain insight into the needs of students and their families that
      might impact negatively on students' progress.
   j. Demonstrates effective consultation techniques that improve
      the quality of professional services provided to students and
      their parents.

Suggested "Pats on the Back"

This section is geared to provide you with ideas for choosing just the
right words to applaud exemplary performance. We hope you will have
cause to make liberal use of these "pats on the back."

   1. Thank you for providing such excellent health service to our
      school. Staff and students' needs are well served as a result of
      your efforts.

   2. Your willingness to (state service that was performed) in spite
      of your busy schedule is very much appreciated. Your exper-
      tise helps our classroom teachers infuse health study into their
      curriculum.

   3. You are a resource for us because of your expertise, attention
      to duty, and willingness to (cooperate, share) your time and
      knowledge.

   4. Your dedicated service contributes to the physical and mental
      health of staff and students. They all benefit from knowing that
      their health concerns are being addressed.

   5. Our school is well-served as a result of your work as a pivotal
      member of the Child Study Team.

   6. Your work in diagnosing, assessing, and servicing students who
      are (academically, behaviorally, emotionally) challenged is
      exceptional.

7. You possess and use your in-depth knowledge of (special education law, Individuals With Disabilities Education Act [IDEA], school and state health codes, etc.) to the best advantage of the staff and students.

8. Your professional and calming manner assists parents to (articulate, alleviate) their (concerns, fears, questions) regarding their child's (health, mental health, behavior, academics) and/or other developmental problems.

9. Our staff, students, and parents are comforted by the confidentiality with which you work with their (cases, records, medical information, personal data). This is a hallmark of your professionalism.

10. In addition to providing care and attention to our students and staff, you use your knowledge and skills to assist them to monitor and improve their health.

Section VI

MAINTENANCE PERSONNEL

Boiler Operator, Food Service Manager and Worker, Head Custodian, Custodian

This section assists the administrator in determining if basic qualifications, expertise, and requirements for successful fulfillment of duties inherent to the job title have been demonstrated.

Performance Statements

Note: With occasional editing, Performance Statements are interchangeable between job titles in this section, when appropriate.

Boiler Operator

A. Specific Tasks
   a. Fires, fuels, and manipulates valves and pressure control gauges and performs all other duties specific to properly operating the boilers.
   b. Fires at proper thickness, regulates draft, and maintains the water at the required level for boiler to run at peak efficiency and safety level.
   c. Performs all relevant tests to boiler water and regulates conditions by using appropriate (equipment, apparatus).
   d. Conducts ongoing (adjustments, maintenance) of all boiler room equipment.
   e. Maintains the boiler and pump room in immaculate condition.
   f. Maintains water in the boiler at the required level.
   g. Demonstrates knowledge of all automatic and manual stokers, pumps, and gauges.
   h. Conducts ongoing inspection of safety devices and related equipment.
   i. Established eligibility for employment by means of successful completion of (required training exercises, tests for knowledge and competency, internship, apprenticeship).

       j. Consistently prepares for and successfully passes all inspections of boiler operation conducted by district supervisory personnel.

B. Level of Expertise
    a. Demonstrates knowledge of the use of electronic and/or manual (equipment, techniques) to (communicate about, maintain, record, perform) job-related tasks.
    b. Demonstrates proficiency in (reading, writing, speaking) skills.
    c. Demonstrates knowledge of terminology specific to the position.
    d. Adept at making (emergency, minor) repairs and maintains equipment in sound operating condition.
    e. Functions at the highest level of competence in the performance of duties, as demonstrated by (describe specific action, using job description and/or clinical observation as basis for comment).
    f. Familiar with the normal operation of blowers, motors, and regulators, and reports malfunction promptly.
    g. Performs emergency (repairs, procedures), where indicated, in order to maintain appropriate levels of boiler function and capability.
    h. Inspects and checks safety (devices, units) and keeps machinery properly cleaned and lubricated.
    i. Has knowledge of the problems, procedures, and methods used in boiler operation, maintenance, and repair.
    j. Has knowledge of proper water level in boilers in order to secure the maximum level of safety and operation.

C. Preparation and Organization
    a. Obtains, stores, safeguards, and properly uses (equipment, material, supplies).
    b. Maintains a sufficient inventory of (materials, supplies, fuel).
    c. Washes boiler and pump rooms and performs other functions in order to maintain the areas in a clean, orderly, and safe condition.
    d. Maintains records and files showing readings of fuel consumption, pressure, draft, temperature, and steam flow.
    e. Completes and submits all reports required by the governing reporting (department, agency).
    f. Conducts simple tests on boiler water to determine the amount of (hardness, acidity, alkalinity), and operates boiler water conditioning apparatus and equipment.
    g. Maintains an accurate (record, inventory) of (requisitions for repair, work orders, schedules of maintenance and repair, purchase orders, etc.).
    h. Keeps the furnace room and surrounding areas free from trash or any combustible material.

    i. Reports to work in sufficient time to ensure that the proper temperature is reached before the arrival of students and staff.

    j. Organizes assigned work and demonstrates sound work (habits, techniques).

D. Related Duties

    a. Notifies proper (persons, authorities) to report (breakage, damage, malfunction, outside interference) with/of furnaces, heaters.

    b. Operates and maintains air conditioning and refrigeration equipment.

    c. (At conclusion of firing season, On a regular basis), (cleans, dusts, polishes) boiler room and surrounding areas.

    d. Keeps essential records and files noting the readings of (fuel consumption, pressure, draft conditions, temperature, steam flow).

    e. Makes minor repairs, cuts and trims grass and shrubbery, and performs related duties.

    f. (Collaborates, Cooperates) with (suppliers, repairmen, etc.) when acquiring needed services.

    g. Demonstrates knowledge of varied types of machines and equipment used in a (power, high-pressure heating) plant.

    h. Seeks additional assistance when indicated by emergency conditions.

    i. Demonstrates ability to fire stationary boilers used in generating power to supply steam to turbines and other steam-powered equipment.

    j. Maintains neat and accurate log sheets detailing the function, maintenance, and repair of equipment.

E. Interpersonal Domain

    a. Performs comparable duties, when requested by authorized authorities.

    b. Secures boiler room area to prevent entry of children or non-authorized personnel.

    c. Responds to (requests, reports) regarding (building, classroom, temperature, function of heating and cooling units) and performs all necessary problem-solving functions.

    d. Seeks feedback from all areas of building as to temperature comfort level and other concerns, where they exist.

    e. Circulates throughout the building in order to personally gauge the temperature and comfort levels.

    f. Adapts (willingly, readily, professionally) to changes in (work schedule, duty assignments, assigned school, etc.) when and if they occur.

    g. (Works with, Shares expertise with, Trains) boiler workers during their (training, internship, apprenticeship) periods.

h. (Open to, Willingly participates in) continuing training opportunities related to the position.

i. Establishes a sound rapport with staff and remains open to (comments, suggestions) regarding the temperature conditions within their work areas.

j. Performs duties in a manner that ensures the safety and comfort of students and staff.

Food Service Manager and Worker

A. Specific Tasks

a. Develops and adheres to time schedules for the delivery of food and lunch services to students and staff.

b. Maintains an inventory of consumable food supplies.

c. Reports (conditions, incidences) that impact negatively on health and/or safety factors in (lunchroom, cafeteria, lavatories, and surrounding areas).

d. Follows (instructions, directives) issued regarding (special diets, allergies, health issues) of identified students.

e. Inspects lunchroom for (hazards, sanitary conditions) prior to the start of food service activities.

f. Assists in monitoring sound eating practices at assigned tables and/or areas.

g. Follows (school, district) prescribed method of delivery of food services.

h. Reads, interprets, and monitors gauges on (refrigerators, freezers, heating units) to ensure that foods are (maintained, heated, cooked) at proper temperatures.

i. Counts and inventories deliveries for correct count.

j. (Requests, Reports) needed repair of (malfunctioning, obsolete, broken) equipment.

B. Level of Expertise

a. Inspects (packaged lunches, buffet food, produce items, etc.) before serving in order to ensure that health code standards are met.

b. Prepares food service area for inspection.

c. Is (proactive, professional, creative) in meeting the needs of students and staff such as (describe extra measures taken to provide excellent service).

d. Shares information regarding special conditions with fellow workers.

e. Prepares clear, neat, and accurate requisitions for food supplies and food preparation equipment.

f. (Knowledgeable of, Skilled in) operating (appliances, machinery) used for on-site food preparation.

  g. Knowledgeable of required health and safety practices for food service personnel.
  h. Maintains comprehensive records and files of job-related data.
  i. Operates (food service, revenue-collecting, record-keeping, etc.) equipment, machinery with skill and accuracy.
  j. Prepares and serves (special diets, menus) under the direction of school physician and/or nurse.

C. Preparation and Organization
  a. Maintains a neat and clean appearance.
  b. Dresses appropriately in order to perform the physical duties of the position.
  c. Maintains a sound record of attendance.
  d. Reports to work in a timely manner.
  e. Anticipates need and takes action to replenish food items in order to maintain the smooth flow of food service.
  f. Adopts and maintains good personal health and hygiene.
  g. Willingly wears appropriate clothing, head gear, and other apparel and footwear required by the district.
  h. Consistently utilizes effective supplies and equipment geared for the maintenance of health and safety conditions in the food service area/s.
  i. Demonstrates knowledge of all (terminology, rules and regulations, etc.) specific to the position.
  j. Prepares job-related (reports, lists, memorandum) where needed.

D. Related Duties
  a. (Posts, Follows) (daily, weekly) lunch (schedules, menus).
  b. Inspects food service area to determine health, safety, and hygienic conditions.
  c. Inspects sanitary condition of lavatories nearest to food service area.
  d. Posts (sanitary code, inspection reports) and other documents supporting evidence of compliance with statea and district codes.
  e. Participates in orientation and educational programs provided by the school and district.
  f. Collects, counts, and maintains record of all monies paid at point of service for food items.
  g. Prepares school lunches for students going on field trips.
  h. Transports and retrieves school lunches to and from classrooms or other designated areas.
  i. Maintains records and files relating to (food preparation, service, costs, inventory, personnel).
  j. Adheres to all required standards, policies, and procedures concerning the (inspection, storage, preparation, service) of food.

E. Interpersonal Domain
   a. Aware of dietary restrictions of students.
   b. Maintains food service area in a neat and sanitary condition.
   c. Adjusts work schedule to accommodate school (emergency closings, ½ sessions, delayed openings).
   d. Seeks opinions from staff and students regarding (food menu, cafeteria service, physical plant, etc.) and acts on constructive suggestions.
   e. (Projects, Maintains) an air of (congeniality, friendliness, warmth, etc.) to students and staff when performing his or her duties.
   f. Collaborates with other workers and custodial staff to inspect, review, and remedy all negative health and sanitary conditions in the cafeteria and surrounding areas.
   g. (Cooperates with, Works well with) fellow workers and other school staff.
   h. Acts on constructive suggestions with grace and effectiveness.
   i. Performs as a viable, contributing member of the school staff.

Head Custodian, Custodian

A. Specific Tasks
   a. Successfully completed all qualifying criteria for obtaining the position.
   b. (Secures, Obtains) required supplies and equipment, using district-approved methods.
   c. (Demonstrates the ability, Is willing) to make minor repairs that do not require (requisitions, work orders, licensed workmen).
   d. Demonstrates knowledge of the safe and efficient procedures involved in loading, unloading supplies and equipment.
   e. Adheres to all required district procedures when (filing reports, recording data, communicating information) regarding school conditions.
   f. Performs all (required, assigned) duties on school (property, grounds).
   g. Disposes of waste materials in a safe, neat, and healthful manner.
   h. (Orders, Requests, Anticipates the need for) necessary supplies and equipment.
   i. (Complies with, Responds to) requests for services in areas of responsibility.
   j. Willingly performs assigned, as well as other reasonable custodial duties, including (replacing light bulbs, servicing water coolers, mowing lawns, trimming hedges, raking and burning leaves, trimming driveway and sidewalk edges, clearing staff parking lot, shoveling snow from driveway, sidewalk, spreading sand, rock salt on icy surfaces, etc.).

B. Level of Expertise
  a. Demonstrates degree of physical fitness necessary for fulfilling the requirements of job activities.
  b. Pays attention to detail in the performance of duty.
  c. Operates (motor vehicle, fork lift, equipment) in a skilled and safe manner.
  d. Demonstrates the ability to understand and carry out oral and/or written directions.
  e. Seeks to (advance, enhance) (knowledge, position) through advanced study or training, in order to meet higher qualifying standards.
  f. Cleans, alone or with others, large areas, including (offices, cafeterias, halls, gymnasiums, auditorium, lavatories, etc.)
  g. Maximizes effectiveness and longevity of supplies and equipment through prudent use and care.
  h. Replenishes and services consumables, including (water coolers, air conditioner filters, etc.), where indicated.
  i. Is mechanically inclined.
  j. Possesses a sense of (aesthetic, organizational) awareness, as demonstrated by the conditions maintained in assigned work areas.

C. Preparation and Organization
  a. Maintains a good attendance record.
  b. (Apportions, Manages) time so as to complete all assigned duties during his or her shift.
  c. Maximizes productivity by working in an organized and sequential manner.
  d. Works efficiently and productively, without direction and/or supervision.
  e. Consistently reports to work on time.
  f. Stores equipment, materials, and supplies, and maintains work areas in a clean and orderly manner.
  g. Serves as model for using sound practices and procedures, and assists new hires to (adopt, duplicate, learn) productive methods and techniques.
  h. Maintains (log, checklist) of (required, completed) tasks.
  i. Requests assistance, where needed, for areas that require (special, concentrated) services.
  j. Uses (skills, knowledge, experience) gained from participating in training sessions to enhance job performance.

D. Related Duties
  a. Reports to alternate sites to perform duties, where required.
  b. Demonstrates an ability to utilize various types of technical, automatic, and/or manual equipment in the performance of (routine, specialized) tasks.

   c. Upon request, picks up (parts, materials, supplies, mail, packages, messages, etc.) from central (storage facility, office).
   d. Inspects and maintains order in (lavatories, locker room, lunchroom).
   e. Investigates incidences of (vandalism, tampering, trespassing) to (authority in charge, law enforcement agency, central office).
   f. (Able to perform, Familiar with) the tasks of other workers of the same title.
   g. Open to constructive (feedback, comments) made by (administration, reporting agency, personnel) and makes necessary adjustments in a timely and efficient manner.
   h. Delivers school lunches and other supplies and equipment to designated areas.
   i. Works at other school locations, when required.
   j. Participates in major schoolwide (cleaning, maintenance) activities during (summer, vacation) period.

E. Interpersonal Domain
   a. Upon request, assumes additional duties necessitated by (emergency situations, absence of other staff).
   b. (Establishes, Maintains) a collegial relationship with (other workers, supervisor, staff).
   c. Assumes responsibility for maintaining assigned areas.
   d. Maintains decorum and demonstrates a professional demeanor.
   e. Enjoys a relationship of mutual respect with (administrators, students, staff, parents, fellow workers, tradesmen).
   f. Maintains a neat appearance.
   g. While on duty, takes measures to safely secure all items of value found in assigned areas.
   h. Seeks feedback on performance and accepts and acts upon constructive suggestions.
   i. Is proactive in making minor repairs and performing non-mandated duties, where needed.
   j. Assists (tradesmen, technicians, etc.) in (carrying tools, materials, placing and removing ladders and supports, cleaning work areas after job is completed).

Suggested "Pats on the Back"

This section is geared to provide you with ideas for choosing just the right words to applaud exemplary performance. We hope you will have cause to make liberal use of these "pats on the back."

   1. We can point to (name of school) with pride because of your efforts. Your pride in the building is evident.

2. Your timely and effective response to requests for services from the staff is acknowledged and appreciated. You perform your duties with pride and competence.

3. You do more than do your work. You do it right! Thank you for your efforts.

4. Your love of (name of school), its staff and students, is evident in the excellence of your work.

5. It is evident that you feel a sense of responsibility for maintaining the well-being and comfort of our students and staff.

6. You perform your duties with care, thoroughness, and helpfulness. We benefit from your sense of duty.

7. You play a (very important, pivotal) role in the functioning of the school. We depend on you for maintaining our clean and orderly environment.

8. You work to ensure that our building is sanitary, comfortable, and conducive to teaching and learning.

9. Your dependability and accommodating manner make it a joy to have you on the staff of (name of school). You set the standard for (job performance, accomplishment) for others.

10. Allow me to commend you on the responsible way in which you perform your duties. We benefit from your dedication.

Section VII

SECURITY STAFF

Driver Education, Traffic Safety Personnel, Police Officer, Security Guard

This section assists the administrator in determining if basic qualifications, expertise, and requirements for successful fulfillment of duties inherent to the job title have been demonstrated.

Performance Statements

Note: With occasional editing, Performance Statements are interchangeable between job titles in this section, when appropriate.

Driver Education, Traffic Safety Personnel

A. Specific Tasks
   a. Provides in-class instruction, including (consumer education topics, vehicle ownership, driver liability insurance).
   b. Provides in-class instruction, including (rules of the road, state traffic laws, local traffic ordinances, signs, signals, highway markings, design) and all other topics necessary for efficient and safe driving performance.
   c. (Teaches, Demonstrates) strategies for defensive driving.
   d. Exhibits teaching abilities that are essential to successful performance as a driver and traffic safety education teacher.
   e. Possesses a valid driver's license to operate vehicles being used and has a satisfactory driving record, as identified by the state.
   f. (Works within, Upholds) all district-mandated guidelines geared to protect students and school personnel from (personal liability, injury, etc.).
   g. Collaborates with school administration in evaluating and improving the effectiveness of driver education, traffic safety education.
   h. Assists students to meet school regulations and state licensing requirements.

     i. (Demonstrates, Illustrates, Teaches) essential driving maneuvers and fundamental (perceptual, judgmental, decision-making, defensive-driving) skills.

     j. (Identifies, Teaches) the physical and psychological characteristics that relate to driving performance.

B. Level of Expertise

     a. Provides real and/or simulated driving experiences, including (night, expressway, rural, urban, suburban, inclement weather) conditions.

     b. Prepares, shares, and discusses data based on (insurance, actuarial, mortality, medical, rehabilitation) statistics, as they relate to the consequences of driving accidents.

     c. (Coordinates, Incorporates) the inclusion of the basic skills into the academic segment of driver and safety education.

     d. Conducts ongoing evaluations of program objectives to determine the extent to which lesson objectives are met.

     e. (Measures, Determines) program outcomes and student performance on the basis of data that have been appropriately collected, analyzed, and interpreted.

     f. Completed an approved program in driver education, traffic safety education and is (credentialed, certified) by the state education agency.

     g. Knowledgeable of the strengths and limitations of highway safety programs.

     h. Utilizes technology that allows students to experience "virtual reality" driving experiences.

     i. Demonstrates knowledge of the operation and safety regulations governing a variety of motor vehicles, including (motorcycles, bicycles, recreational vehicles, commercial vehicles).

     j. Teaches basic mechanics and emergency self-help procedures, including (changing tires, repairing hoses, etc.).

C. Preparation and Organization

     a. Maintains a professional lending library of current publications and periodicals relevant to the subject and course.

     b. Maintains a library of videotapes and utilizes them to give students the opportunity to critique varied elements of safe driving practices.

     c. Maintains record of vehicle (maintenance, repair, purchases).

     d. Develops and has available maintenance records for each motor vehicle used for instruction.

     e. (Takes, Sends) vehicle through inspection and takes appropriate steps to have needed repairs done, where indicated.

     f. Maintains a professional library of current (periodicals, publications, software, media) that are made accessible to students and staff.

g. Maximizes the use of allotted budget to conduct the program, keeping comprehensive records of expenditures and all other transactions.

h. Conducts an ongoing review of the (registration, insurance, maintenance) status on all vehicles used for instruction, in order to ensure compliance with regulations.

i. Posts (models, posters) of all working parts of motor vehicles as a part of in-class instruction.

j. Keeps up-to-date with new instructional materials and techniques.

D. Related Duties

a. Prepares, analyzes, and interprets (evaluation results, performance analyses) of course effectiveness.

b. Monitors students' records to ensure they meet minimum requirements adopted by school authorities for enrollment in driver's education course.

c. Conducts field trip to (inspection station, DMV agency, rehabilitation hospitals, traffic court, etc.) in order to provide students with authentic driver experiences.

d. Collaborates with the school nurse in screening students for possible physical and/or psychological limitations prior to commencing actual in-car instruction.

e. Makes appropriate modifications to instruction to accommodate students with special needs.

f. Bases in-car instruction on the appropriate diagnosis of students' (developmental characteristics, learning style, knowledge, skill level).

g. Informs students of career opportunities in the field of (highway safety, driving).

h. Emphasizes the negative effects of alcohol and other drugs on driving performance.

i. Teaches techniques of coping with adverse environmental conditions while driving.

j. (Stresses, Promotes) the importance of being a responsible driver.

E. Interpersonal Domain

a. Emphasizes personal (responsibility, liability) to students, including (behavioral patterns, e.g., the dangers of "road rage" or driving while impaired or tired, defensive driving, respect for traffic laws and law enforcement, wearing seat belt, etc.).

b. Seeks (grants, contributions, donations) of used cars and other resources to enhance the driver and traffic safety education program.

c. Is conscious of the impact that the driving experiences have on students' sense of accomplishment and self-worth.

d. Stresses the need to maintain vehicle in a functional, safe, clean, and properly maintained condition.

e. Prepares written notification to parents regarding the program, including (program description and activities, school and district legal responsibilities, criteria for successful completion of program).

f. (Volunteers for, Participates in) community driving/traffic safety activities.

g. Teaches students respect for existing laws governing pedestrian rights.

h. Maintains appropriate relationship with (traffic officials, community groups, media) in order to gain support for the traffic safety education program.

i. Invites (local law enforcement, medical personnel, etc.) to lecture, conduct demonstrations, advise) students about driving/traffic safety.

j. Seeks to obtain adequate (technical assistance, funding) from district and state educational agencies.

Police Officer

A. Specific Tasks

a. Patrols assigned areas in order to protect the welfare and property of students and staff.

b. Reports to scene of accidents and acts to obtain needed aid for injured parties.

c. Under the direction of the school administration, makes arrests and transports offenders to police station.

d. Cooperates with (school security, administrators) to (question, stop, detain) suspicious persons, obtain their ID, and make a determination as to the validity of their presence in the building.

e. Reports to scene of (incidents, emergencies) and takes appropriate action, including (blocking area, standing guard, preventing undue damage, loss, injury) and all other actions, as warranted.

f. (Examines, Inspects) documents, including student ID, to determine authenticity and ownership.

g. Maintains an (appropriate, high) level of physical, mental, and emotional strength.

h. Enlists the aid of (fellow officers, school security) in the apprehension of suspects/perpetrators.

i. Receives reports, descriptions of (suspects, trespassers, theft, violence, etc.) by radio transmission, and responds accordingly.

j. Seeks to (neutralize volatile situations, disarm persons, etc.) by adopting a calm but authoritative (presence, demeanor, attitude).

B. Level of Expertise
   a. Knowledgeable in the operation of manual and mechanical emergency first-aid methods, equipment, including (defibrillators, oxygen masks, first-aid kits, etc.).
   b. Possesses (peace-keeping, counseling, calming) abilities.
   c. Maintains observation of persons suspected of unlawful activity and notifies (administration, superiors, school security guards) in order to conduct appropriate follow-up.
   d. Adept at conducting (interviews, investigations), and logs statements, facts, and evidence when writing reports.
   e. Secures evidence at scene of (accidents, incidents) in order to prevent evidence from being overlooked and/or destroyed.
   f. Where required, testifies in court, utilizing required documents, reports, and other evidence and relevant documentation.
   g. Adept in the use of all (electronic, manual) computer technology and related software relevant to the performance of duty.
   h. Assesses situations by utilizing information received from (school authorities, staff, students, parents, witnesses).
   i. (Makes presentations, Participates in discussions) on a variety of topics related to (police work, student behaviors, criminal, juvenile justice systems) to (classes, individuals, small or large groups).
   j. Promotes law enforcement as a viable career choice to the students.

C. Preparation and Organization
   a. Maintains equipment, including (flashlight, walkie-talkie, scanner wand, etc.) in working order.
   b. Reports to duty in full uniform, reads all relevant reports, and shares information with fellow officers, in order to maintain continuity of service.
   c. Inventories and maintains equipment, supplies issued to department; replaces missing or damaged items to ensure readiness for use.
   d. Develops reports and files.
   e. (Records, Logs) activities by completing log sheets, including duty rosters, activities, incidents encountered, and all other relevant notations.
   f. Constructs timely, legible, and highly accurate reports.
   g. Knowledgeable of current laws, procedures, and trends governing (search-and-seizure activities, use of force, student rights, arrest procedures).
   h. Maintains issued uniform and equipment by obtaining cleaning, repair, and restorative services, in order to ensure proper personal appearance and serviceability of equipment.

    i. Maintains a current list of telephone numbers for (emergency, social service, juvenile justice) services and agencies.

    j. Has knowledge of membership, affiliation, and activities of (street gangs, former offenders, bullies, etc.).

D. Related Duties

    a. (Assists, Serves as back-up to) school security personnel in the performance of their duties.

    b. Separates parties involved in altercations, disperses crowds, and escorts combatants to (administrative, guidance, medical) office.

    c. Conducts (interviews, investigations) of crime scenes, and (develops, analyzes, communicates, interprets) findings.

    d. Regulates and controls pedestrian and vehicular movement in order to ensure a smooth traffic flow as well as pedestrian safety.

    e. In the course of performing duty, reports unsafe, unusual, and/or hazardous conditions.

    f. Responds to complaints of (misconduct, illegal activity, hazardous condition, etc.) in a timely and effective manner.

    g. Uses approved techniques in all incidences of human contact.

    h. Issues (summonses, tickets, warnings), where indicated, for violations of school and district rules regarding (describe infraction).

    i. Assists in the evacuation of the building during (fire drills, emergencies, emergency evacuation drills, etc.) and facilitates safe reentry.

    j. Communicates (in person, by telephone) with parents regarding police incidents involving their children.

E. Interpersonal Domain

    a. Calms volatile situations by listening to, validating, and reasoning with all involved parties.

    b. Enjoys positive interaction with (staff, students, parents, community) in an atmosphere of mutual respect.

    c. Promotes good will by (respectful demeanor, sound communication skills, validating the concerns of others, etc.) and by gaining the confidence and support of students, staff, and the community.

    d. Locates and questions witnesses.

    e. (Knowledgeable of, Respectful of) the (customs, concerns, beliefs) of the students, staff, and community, and validates their diversity.

    f. Works well within the greater community as well as in the school.

    g. (Responds, Reacts) with quiet and professional authority when confronted with (volatile, stressful) situations.

    h. Assumes a leadership role where and when needed, in the performance of duty.

i. (Accepts, Acts upon) (suggestions, leads, tips, information) supplied by responsible students, staff and maintains the confidentiality of the provider.

j. Enjoys a (professional, collaborative, productive) relationship with school security personnel.

Security Guard

A. Specific Tasks

a. Patrols assigned areas and visually and manually inspects the (physical plant, surroundings) in order to ensure that building is secure and free from (trespassers, vandalism, unlawful entry, hazards, etc.).

b. Inspects area for conditions that might contribute to fire and determines if the fire extinguishers are in place and operational.

c. Remains at post and manages the flow of individuals entering and/or exiting the building.

d. (Obtains, Requests) verbal or written information from visitors pertaining to their intended destination, identification, and nature of visit.

e. (Deters, Restrains, Removes) all persons behaving (innappropriately, violently, suspiciously) and who cause disturbances that impede regular school proceedings.

f. Communicates with central headquarters, administrators, and other security officers concerning the performance of duties.

g. Enforces no- (smoking, loitering, trespassing) rules and regulations.

h. Thoroughly inspects students' identification and conducts searches of (persons, property) at point of entry before admitting into the building.

i. Demonstrates the physical, mental, and emotional ability to perform the required duties of the position.

j. Maintains order and discipline among students.

B. Level of Expertise

a. Identifies staff, students, and/or visitors entering or leaving the building by means of facial recognition.

b. (Is alert to, Recognizes on sight) persons (trespassing, entering, present) in the building without authorization.

c. Adept in the use of various types of electronic and/or manual recording and information systems and computer technology.

d. Able to understand and carry out oral and written directions without (supervision, direction).

e. Has working knowledge of school law as it pertains to student rights and/or responsibilities.

f. (Seeks to obtain, Possesses) a basic knowledge of (first aid, CPR, Heimlich maneuver, etc.).

g. Attends and fully participates in all mandated job-related training sessions.

h. Knowledgeable of (court, juvenile and criminal justice, truancy) procedures.

i. Knowledgeable of current security (laws, procedures, trends, practices, methods, equipment) and utilizes knowledge to increase effectiveness and productivity.

j. Operates (elevators, body scanning devices, fire extinguishers) for security and/or safety purposes.

C. Preparation and Organization

a. Maintains a neat and orderly sign-in book.

b. Records visits to watch stations at specified intervals, indicating that rounds have been completed.

c. Reports (malfunctioning, missing equipment, hazardous conditions, evidence of theft, vandalism, etc.) to reporting authority.

d. Maintains radio communication with (headquarters, school authorities) by operating walkie-talkie properly and under suitable circumstances.

e. Prepares clear, accurate, comprehensive, and legible reports of conditions noted and actions taken.

f. Organizes routine assignments and maintains effective work habits.

g. Maintains required uniform and equipment at peak level of cleanliness and operation.

h. Participates in roll call and is attentive to announcements regarding (work assignments, central office news, etc.)

i. Reports promptly and works effectively when (temporarily assigned to other schools or locations, calls for assistance are made, etc.).

j. Maintains a good attendance and punctuality record.

D. Related Duties

a. Makes court appearances in order to testify in cases of (vandalism, theft, misconduct, arson, etc.).

b. Checks the perimeters of school grounds for (parking violations, trespassers, hazardous conditions, loiterers) and takes appropriate action.

c. Checks cars in (reserved, restricted) parking areas and issues (warnings, citations) to prevent, deter future use by unauthorized individuals.

d. Seizes (contraband, illegal, stolen) (property, material) and detains suspects for questioning and further investigation.

e. Is proactive in initiating preventative action that deters incidents from occurring.

  f. Performs security duties at off-site school functions, including (sports events, field trips, public arenas, etc.), when assigned.

  g. Accompanies staff and students, whenever necessary, to ensure their (safe passage, freedom from incident).

  h. Searches and/or secures packages that might contain dangerous and/or contraband items.

  i. Able to write clear and concise letters, reports, descriptions, and/or instructions.

  j. Able to sustain productivity in the light of needed physical exertion, stress, and responsibility associated with the position.

 E. Interpersonal Domain

  a. (Cooperates, Collaborates) with assigned police officers.

  b. Provides accurate information regarding the location of persons, areas, and services offered in the building.

  c. Enjoys a relationship of mutual respect with students, staff, and the community.

  d. Listens and responds to concerns voiced by neighbors of the school, including (homeowners, merchants, community members, etc.)

  e. Seeks feedback regarding job performance and acts on constructive suggestions in a mature and timely manner.

  f. Demonstrates the ability to work harmoniously with associates, staff, visitors, and all other persons conducting school business.

  g. Displays a courteous, but firm demeanor.

  h. Demonstrates the ability to be polite and helpful when dealing with staff, students, and the public.

  i. Handles (disrespect, verbal abuse, criticism, goading, stress) with patience, calm, maturity, and professionalism.

  j. Uses position of authority with appropriate restraint and courtesy.

Suggested "Pats on the Back"

This section is geared to provide you with ideas for choosing just the right words to applaud exemplary performance. We hope you will have cause to make liberal use of these "pats on the back."

1. The staff and students of (name of school) work in a safe and secure environment because of your efforts. Education thrives in the environment you help maintain.

2. Your calm, but authoritative presence has (averted, calmed, soothed) potential crisis situations. Your experience and professionalism is appreciated.

3. (Name of school) prides itself on the safe and secure climate in which our staff and students work. Thank you for contributing to this productive learning environment.

4. Because of your efforts, our students emerge as responsible and skillful motorists. Thank you for being exacting and unwavering in your standards for their successful achievement.

5. Your services in (preventing and managing school violence, reducing risk of liability, improving school-community relations) are valued. Thank you for your efforts.

6. Your training, experience, and dedication to the job are evident in the manner in which you protect the staff and students. You are a valued member of the school family.

7. The care and attention you expend with the students will reap dividends in the future in the form of avoided injuries and saved lives.

8. The student body relates to you as a friend and protector who deserves respect and cooperation. This speaks to the quality of your professionalism and caring for our students.

9. Thank you for your reliability and focused job performance! The administration, staff, and students of (name of school) benefit from your efforts.

10. Students thrive in an environment in which they feel safe and secure. Please continue with the excellent job performance that makes that possible.

ADMINISTRATION

Assistant or Vice Principal, Principal

This section assists the administrator in determining if basic qualifications, expertise, and requirements for successful fulfillment of duties inherent to the job title have been demonstrated.

Performance Statements

Note: With occasional editing, Performance Statements are interchangeable between job titles in this section, when appropriate.

Assistant or Vice Principal

A. Specific Tasks
   a. Communicates effectively with (staff, students, parents, community, outside agencies, etc.).
   b. Assists in the implementation of program initiatives through the development of appropriate professional develop opportunities for staff.
   c. (Articulates, Upholds, Supports) the philosophy, mission, and direction of the school (program, principal).
   d. Assists in the completion of performance evaluations of the school (programs, staff) and initiates needed improvements.
   e. (Oversees, Monitors) the developing progress of staff in carrying out activities in their Professional Improvement Plans (PIPs).
   f. Assists in the (preparation, management) of (schedules, budgets, curriculum, instruction).
   g. Manages a range of supplementary duties, including (hiring and monitoring substitute teachers, ensuring building security, supervising non-instructional services and providers, etc.).
   h. Assumes all duties, responsibilities designated by the principal and serves as acting principal, when needed.
   i. (Interviews, Recommends, Trains, Orients, Supervises, Evaluates) instructional and non-instructional staff.

      j. Assists in providing direction to staff in implementing (instructional, school, district) goals and objectives.

  B. Level of Expertise
      a. Possesses the desire and ability to engage in continuing education and related pursuits geared to upgrade professional skills.
      b. Maintains a comprehensive knowledge of (laws, regulations, new techniques, practices, trends, advances) in the educational profession.
      c. (Participates in, Develops, Assesses) the program of professional development for staff.
      d. Demonstrates the ability to interpret student achievement test results and to communicate same to (students, teachers, parents).
      e. Acts to upgrade personal professional knowledge and skills.
      f. Communicates and carries out established school program goals, objectives, and policies.
      g. Delegates and accepts responsibility for the timely and accurate completion of tasks.
      h. Serves on (school, district) committees and represents the school's best interests.
      i. Assists in grant writing.
      j. Ensures that the instructional objectives are developed and involves faculty in the (planning, implementation) of (program, curriculum) initiatives.

  C. Preparation and Organization
      a. (Possesses, Effectively utilizes) a range of communication modes to reach students, staff, and parents.
      b. Assists the principal in maintaining a safe, orderly, positive, and effective learning environment.
      c. Completes all required (reports, documents) in an accurate and timely manner.
      d. Maintains financial records with accuracy.
      e. Develops a system to (organize, handle, keep current with, complete, accomplish) administrative tasks such as (student and teacher records, attendance procedures, purchasing, budgets, schedules, evaluations, etc.).
      f. (Manages, Directs, Maintains) records on the materials, supplies, equipment) used to carry out the daily school program of activities.
      g. Requisitions and allocates supplies, equipment, and instructional material, as needed.
      h. Coordinates and oversees the day-to-day operation of the school.
      i. Operates a computer to (retrieve, enter, and review information, word process, compile data, maintain files, develop

spreadsheets, desktop publish) and to accomplish other administrative tasks.

   j. Reads professional literature and (attends conferences, seminars, workshops, training sessions, etc.).

D. Related Duties

   a. Assists staff in the creation of effective professional development plans.

   b. Assists in the identification of staffing needs for the school and assists in selection of staff.

   c. (Contributes to, Oversees, Monitors) the publication of the school (Web page, newsletter, brochures, etc.).

   d. (Prepares, Completes) various (forms, reports, correspondence, schedules, contracts, programs, instructional materials, news releases, flyers, brochures, claim forms, accident or incident reports, etc.).

   e. Assists in the preparation and monitors the school program budget, purchasing, and inventory.

   f. Works cooperatively with the (principal, assistant superintendent, program coordinators, supervisors, etc.) to coordinate the school program of instruction.

   g. Assists in conducting student (orientation, scheduling, registration, etc.) operations.

   h. Shares the duty of supervising (evening, afterschool, sports, off-site, etc.) student activities.

   i. Monitors the testing program.

   j. Initiatives programs to (highlight, honor, recognize, showcase) staff and student achievement.

E. Interpersonal Domain

   a. Demonstrates the ability to work effectively within a team environment.

   b. Exhibits (multicultural awareness, gender sensitivity, racial and ethnic appreciation).

   c. Involves staff in setting budget priorities.

   d. Defines and disseminates information about the school (mission, disciplinary policies and procedures) to parents, students, staff, and the community.

   e. (Communicates, Works) (effectively, productively) with (administration, staff, support personnel, parents, agencies, community) and all others when conducting school-related business.

   f. (Promotes, Maintains) open communication with students, staff, and parents.

   g. Promotes positive student attitudes and respects the dignity and value of staff and students.

   h. Supports (school, student, staff) initiatives by attending (off-site events, sports program events, social events, etc.).

     i. Demonstrates moral and ethical judgment and behaviors.

     j. Works collegially and effectively with the principal.

Principal

A. Specific Tasks

    a. Organizes, manages, evaluates, and supervises procedures for the operation and function of the school, in a manner consistent with the philosophy, mission, values, goals, and objectives of the school and district.

    b. Supervises the instructional program of the school, evaluating lesson plans and observing classes on an ongoing basis.

    c. Ensures that the program of instruction engages the learners in (tasks, activities, experiences) that represent the best practices in the field of education.

    d. Organizes and nurtures an effective leadership team of (assistants, grade-level representatives, department chairpersons) with clear expectations for their roles, responsibilities, and performance.

    e. Provides opportunities for effective staff development that addresses the needs of the (instructional program, school), including (workshops, conferences, visitations, inservice sessions).

    f. Organizes and supervises all programs that support the school curriculum mandates, including the program of (athletics, extracurricular activities, etc.).

    g. Develops, recommends, and submits a budget for the operation of the school and approves all (purchases, acquisitions) in accordance with school and district regulations.

    h. Assumes responsibility for the health, safety, and welfare of students, staff, and visitors.

    i. Accounts for the (maintenance, use, auditing) of all school funds, including (student activity costs, graduation fees, collections, fundraising proceeds, etc.).

    j. Stresses the importance of sound parental involvement.

B. Level of Expertise

    a. (Familiar with, Knowledgeable of, Endorses, Includes school initiatives supportive of) the principles of the federal 2001 No Child Left Behind (law, policy, legislation) and other related educational mandates for student achievement.

    b. (Enjoys, Develops) a personal (mission, vision, plan, mandate) for the school and (communicates, shares) those expectations with staff.

    c. Knowledgeable of a variety of instructional strategies and materials, consistent with (traditional, proven, current) research on learning and child growth and development.

d. (Demonstrates, Possesses) effective (communication, presentation) skills when addressing (staff, students, the community, parents, small and large groups, etc.).

e. Engages in ongoing professional growth initiatives through (collaboration with colleagues, membership in professional organizations, attendance at conferences, workshops, seminars, etc.).

f. Adheres to (school and state laws, Board of Education policies and procedures, school regulations, contractual obligations, etc.).

g. (Collects data on, Makes ongoing observations of) teacher performance, utilizing a variety of methods, including (professional activity, peer review, student achievement, action research, systematic observations, school improvement participation and/or outcomes).

h. Adept in the practice of conducting (formative, summative) assessments and other monitoring functions.

i. (Conversant with, Knowledgeable of, Models) the best practices of past and current educational theory, e.g., Dr. Madeline Hunter, etc.

j. (Initiates, Develops) comprehensive technology training for teachers and facilitates participation through the use of (flexible scheduling, support, business partnerships) and other incentives.

C. Preparation and Organization

a. Complies with all laws, administrative codes, board policies, procedures, and regulations.

b. (Approves, Maintains, Develops) a master schedule for the delivery of (instruction, support services, etc.).

c. Completes accurate, comprehensive, and timely (reports, records).

d. Communicates regularly with the district superintendent regarding the school's (needs, successes, general operation, test results, health and safety issues, maintenance concerns, staffing, etc.).

e. Provides procedures for the safe (handling, storing) and integrity of all school records.

f. Operates electronic, computer, and all other equipment needed to carry out administrative (functions, duties).

g. Maintains a system of monitoring and assessing student progress by means of reviewing student (achievement test results, report cards, action research, teacher evaluations, etc.) and all other related data.

h. Conducts meetings, as necessary, for the proper functioning of the school.

i. Develops, communicates, and monitors emergency procedures and practices, including (fire drills, terrorist attack plan, emergency evacuation, etc.).

        j. Remains abreast of all facets of the school's operation through the use of a (viable, comprehensive) reporting system.

  D. Related Duties
      a. Leads school-level planning processes to ensure the development, implementation, and evaluation of school programs and activities, e.g., School-based Management Team, etc.
      b. (Establishes, Implements) procedures for the evaluation and selection of instructional materials and equipment.
      c. Develops and monitors clearly (understood, articulated) emergency procedures and conducts regular drills for compliance with (state, district) guidelines.
      d. Supports and cooperates with the school Parent-Teacher organization.
      e. (Authorizes, Recommends) the (suspension, exclusion, expulsion) from school of any pupil whose (behavior, presence) is detrimental to the health, safety, or welfare of other pupils.
      f. Organizes and supervises procedures for identifying and addressing the special needs of students, including (health-related, physical, emotional, learning, behavioral) disabilities.
      g. Develops a comprehensive program of assistance and support for beginning teachers, including (orientation, mentoring, support groups of peers, informal visitations, formal observations, conferencing, access to teacher-support networks, etc.).
      h. Develops a comprehensive program of assistance and monitoring for teachers (having difficulty, displaying marginal ability), including (data gathering, retraining, etc.).
      i. (Implements, Provides) a program of supplemental services for students, including (tutorial, remedial, afterschool) activities.
      j. Advocates for and represents the best interests of the school when attending (committees, meetings, etc.).

  E. Interpersonal Domain
      a. Conveys information to staff, students, and parents, and establishes and follows procedures for public relations initiatives regarding school (operation, events, achievements).
      b. Maintains visibility and communication with students, staff, and parents.
      c. Attends (school, community) functions in order to demonstrate (support, genuine interest, rapport, accessibility).
      d. (Organizes, Maintains) a public relations system that celebrates and informs parents and the community of the accomplishments of (students, staff, the school).
      e. (Sustains, Establishes, Develops) (a cooperative relationship with, the support of) (parents, the community).

f. Conferences with parents regarding student (progress, lack of progress, behavior, etc.) and all other school-related issues.

g. Maintains a positive, cooperative, and mutually supportive relationship with (central office administration, parents, persons conducting school-related business, agencies, etc.).

h. Provides opportunities for (students, staff) to celebrate success in instructional and non-instructional school (endeavors, activities, etc.).

i. Recognizes teacher and other staff during special Appreciation Days, and throughout the school year.

j. Stresses the importance of healthy parental involvement and (initiates, becomes involved in) practices to promote their (support for, connection to) the school.

Suggested "Pats on the Back"

This section is geared to provide you with ideas for choosing just the right words to applaud exemplary performance. We hope you will have cause to make liberal use of these "pats on the back."

1. At a time when schools are asked to do so much more, (name of school) has met, and surpassed, the challenge. Thank you for your contributions to our success.

2. The fair and objective manner you demonstrate when working with students provides an excellent model for them to emulate when interacting with one another.

3. Your dedication to our staff and students is evident in the support and encouragement you give by attending their (name events, e.g., sports events, science fairs, etc.).

4. Thank you for sharing my vision for (name of school).

5. Thank you for developing a (state-of-the-art professional development program, name specific program) for our staff. Our teachers are motivated and (anxious to begin, fully committed to the program, are benefiting greatly from their participation).

6. Collaboration is key to the productive relationship that we share. I appreciate your dedication to our partnership.

7. School improvement is a reality at (name of school) thanks to your tireless efforts toward implementing a comprehensive professional development (or name other program activity) program. Well done!

8. The students love you; parents admire you; I appreciate you. Keep up the good work!

9. You are one of (name of school) greatest resources due to your tireless efforts and focused vision. Thank you for your commitment to the staff, students, and community.

10. You have made a positive impact on our parent involvement efforts. Parents respond to the genuine concern you demonstrate for their child/ren.

Part II

OTHER HELPFUL RESOURCES FOR WRITING PERFORMANCE EVALUATIONS

VOCABULARY AID

able	arrange	cautious
abusive	arrogant	censure
action	articulate	certainty
acumen	artistic	chaotic
adapt	assess	character
adaptability	assiduous	charming
adaptable	association	checked
add	assortment	clam
adept	assurance	clarity
administer	assure	class
admiration	astute	clean
advance	attempt	clear
adviser	attention	clearness
advocate	attentive	collaborate
aesthetic	attitude	command
affected	audience	comment
affection	augment	compel
aggressive	authority	complete
agreeable	avail self of	compliance
alert	awareness	compliant
alert to	bearing	composure
allegiance	behavior	conceited
allied with	believable	concern
aloof	belittle	concern for
ambitious	beneficial	concerning
amiable	berate	condemn
analyze	bias	conduct
animation	biased	confidence
annoyed	bolster	confirm
anxiety	boost	conformity
aplomb	bright	congenial
appraisal	calm	connection
appraise	capability	contain
appreciate	capable	contribute
approach	care	control
appropriate	careful	cordial
approval	carriage	correlation
ardent	cart	course

courteous	discipline	exploit
covert	discover	exposed
create	discreet	expound
credible	discretion	expression
critical	disordered	fair
criticism	disorderly	fairness
criticize	disparage	faithful
critique	display	familiar
cultured	disposition	fault
cunning	distinguish	faultless
custody	distress	fervent
debonair	divergent	find
deceitful	diverse	flexible
decree	document	force
dedicated	dominant	foreword
dedication	dominate	fortify
deep	drive	friendly
delicate	duty	function
demanding	eager	functioning
demeanor	earnest	gallant
denounce	effective	generous
deportment	effectual	genuine
deprived	effort	giving
design	elegance	grace
desolate	eloquent	grow
detect	emotion	growth
determined	encourage	guarded
develop	endowed	guidance
developed	endurance	guide
devious	energetic	hasten
devoted	energy	heed
diagram	enhance	helpful
dialogue	enlarge	honesty
different	enraged	impact
difficult	equitable	impartial
dignified	equity	impartiality
dignity	erudite	impression
diligent	estimate	improve
diminish	estimation	incisive
diminished	ethical	incite
diplomacy	evaluate	inclination
diplomatic	exact	increase
direct	examine	indulgent
direction	excite	inert
directions	expand	influence
disapprove	expertise	information
discern	explain	infuriated

ingenious	marginal	partake in
initial	masterful	participant
innovative	mastery	passive
insensitive	maximize	pattern of
insight	mediation	pedagogy
insistence	mediocre	pedantic
inspire	member	perceive
instruction	mentor	perception
insufficient	method	perceptive
integrated	meticulous	perfected
integrity	middling	permissive
intellectual	mindful	persistent
intelligent	minimal	persuade
intensify	mission	perturbed
interest	mock	plan
intolerant	model	plans
irate	modeling	pleasant
issue	modest	pliable
joint	modify	pliant
judgment	moral	poise
judgmental	motivate	polite
judicious	multi-faceted	poor
just	multiply	position
justice	negligible	positive
justify	neutrality	potency
keen	notice	power
keen on	nurture	practical
kept	objective	preference
know-how	obnoxious	prejudice
knowledge	observant	prejudiced
leadership	observe	preliminary
learned	obvious	preparation
lenient	occurrence	presence
lesson	open	pretentious
lessons	opinion	produce
lethargic	optimistic	proficiency
liable	order	proficient
logic	orderly	profit from
logical	organized	profound
loquacious	orientation	progress
loyal	original	promise
loyalty	originate	propensity
lucid	outcome	proponent
manage	oversee	protected
manipulate	overt	provisions
manner	pace	provoke
mannerly	painstaking	prudence

pure	serious	thoughtful
purify	sharp	tidy
purpose	shrewd	timely
range	simulation	tolerate
rate	sincere	tonality
rational	sincerity	topic
reaction	skill	toward
readiness	skilled	training
ready	skillful	tranquil
real	slight	translate
reality	sluggish	treatment
reason	smooth	trivial
reasonable	spirit	troubled
rebuke	spirited	tutorial
receptive	stable	unbiased
receptivity	stamina	understand
record	steadfast	unfair
refine	steady	unhelpful
refined	sterile	unified
reform	stimulate	unique
regard for	straight	unjust
related	strange	unpleasant
remark	strength	unrelenting
replica	strengthen	unreliable
reproach	strong	unruly
reserved	studious	unselfish
respect	sturdy	unwary
response	style	value
restrain	substantive	varied
restraint	substitution	variety
result	sufficient	vibrant
reticent	supervise	view
review	supplies	viewpoint
robust	supporter	vigilant
rude	supportive	vigor
rule	survey	vigorous
ruling	system	violent
sagacity	systematic	vivacious
scant	tactics	vivid
scheme	tactless	watch over
scholar	talented	watchful
scholastic	task	willingness
scope of	teaching	wisdom
selfless	technique	wordy
sensible	theme	worried
sensitive	thin	
sequential	thorough	

Section X

THE EVALUATION ORGANIZER

The Evaluation Organizer is offered as a tool to expedite the use of the Guide. Specifically, the organizer sheets and your copy of *Writing Meaningful Evaluations for Non-Instructional Staff—Right Now!!* is all you need as you monitor the delivery of non-instructional performance in your school.

The format of the organizer allows you to use a form of shorthand to record statements that will be used on your approved evaluation instrument. In the example below, we see how the organizer is used to record statements from one of the performance areas for the job title Clerical Staff:

Clerical Staff

B. Level of Expertise

"Pats on the Back"

d	h					5	

We can now decode these Performance Statements as:

d.   -   Assumes a major role in performing office routines and procedures.

h.   -   Is adept in the use of all office technological equipment.

The instructor is also praised by using a statement from the Suggested "Pats on the Back" area located at the end of the section, that is,

5.   -   You are the hub that keeps the spokes of our school wheel in position. You are valued for the role you play.

Evaluation Organizer

Name: _____   Date: __/__/__

Department: _____   Position: _____

Date: ___/___/___   Evaluator: _____

A. Specific Tasks   **"Pats on the Back"**

B. Level of Expertise   **"Pats on the Back"**

C. Preparation and Organization   **"Pats on the Back"**

D. Related Duties   **"Pats on the Back"**

E. Interpersonal Domain   **"Pats on the Back"**

Section XI

RECORD OF EVALUATIONS

Name _____ Title _____ School Year _____

NAME	GRADE	TEN.	NONTEN.	OBSER.	PRE.	EVAL.	POST.
1.							
2.							
3.							
4.							
5.							
6.							
7.							
8.							
9.							
10.							
11.							
12.							
13.							
14.							
15.							
16.							
17.							
18.							
19.							
20.							
21.							
22.							
23.							
24.							

Section XII

A CHECKLIST OF BASIC DOCUMENTATION AND/OR CONDITIONS

Name: _____ Date: ___/___/____

Department/Position: _____

AGENCIES, ORGANIZATIONS

___ Community Leaders
___ Community Organizations
___ Court Departments, Personnel
___ Juvenile Justice
___ School Departments
___ Social Services

ASSESSMENT DATA

___ Achievement Testing
___ Chapter Test
___ IEPs (Individual Educational Plans)
___ Rollbook
___ Student Portfolios
___ Test Data
___ Unit

A-V EQUIPMENT AND SUPPLIES

___ Current Memorandums
___ Flyers/Brochures
___ Inventory
___ Maintenance Record

COMMUNICATION(S)

___ Flyers/Brochures
___ School Newsletter

DIRECTIVES/MEMORANDUMS

___ Emergency Evacuation Plan
___ Fire Drill Plan
___ Meeting Agendas
___ School Rules
___ Seating Chart
___ Substitute Packet (where applicable)

GUIDELINES/POLICIES

___ Codes and Regulations
___ Core Curriculum Standards
___ Department Policies and Procedures
___ Job Description(s)
___ Laws (State/Federal)
___ School Mission Statement

PHYSICAL PLANT

___ Aerated
___ Clean/Aesthetic
___ Effective Use of Space
___ Organization/Neatness

PROFESSIONAL DATA

___ Evaluations
___ Lesson Planbook (where applicable)
___ Long-Range Planning
___ Personal Improvement Plan (PIP)
___ Unit Planning, Thematic Unit)

RECORDS

___ Attendance Records
___ Class/Student List(s)

___ Cumulative Records
___ Financial Statement(s) (where applicable)
___ Inventory:
___ Book
___ Supplies
___ Record of Parental Conferences

REPORTS

___ Accident Reports
___ Insurance/Medical Claims
___ Purchase Orders
___ Requisitions
___ Student Referrals

SCHEDULES

___ Daily Schedule
___ District Calendar
___ Master Schedule
___ Non-Instructional Duties
___ School Monthly Calendar of Events

TEACHING/LEARNING AIDS

___ Bulletin Boards
___ Charts/Posters
___ Curriculum Guides (where applicable)
___ Professional Library
___ Student Reading Library
___ Supplies
___ Teacher's Guides (where applicable)

TECHNOLOGY

___ Computer(s) ___ Software

Section XIII

DESCRIPTION OF POSITIONS

A Brief Overview of the Objectives, Responsibilities, and Tasks Involved in the Job Description

Assistant or Vice Principal

Under the direction of the principal, the assistant or vice principal performs all instructional and non-instructional duties in a management capacity, serving as principal in his or her absence. Responsibilities are diverse, but can be generally described as those that support the principal's vision and/or the school mission.

The assistant or vice principal, as a member of the senior leadership team, must demonstrate a strong educational vision and strategic skills, an understanding of the intellectual and developmental needs of students, and outstanding interpersonal skills.

He or she should possess exemplary teaching experience and must have attained the required administrative certification. Assistant and/or vice principals often possess advanced study on the graduate level.

A short listing of specific responsibilities includes handling discipline, attendance, social and recreational programs, and health and safety conditions.

In addition, the assistant or vice principal plays an important role in developing curriculum, evaluating and planning professional growth initiatives for staff, and furthering school-community relations.

The ability to lead change, contribute to the diverse life of the school community, and work with the principal to achieve the school mission is expected.

Boiler Operator

The boiler operator has sole responsibility for operating and making minor repairs to stationary steam boilers or steam generators, as well as auxiliary boiler equipment. The primary function is to safeguard, monitor, and regulate valves and gauges at the appropriate comfort and safety levels in order to maintain climatic and atmospheric comfort levels in the physical plant.

Counselors

Child Study Team, Guidance, Attendance, Student Assistance

The services provided by these counselors focuses on meeting the individual needs of students who are typically functioning, disaffected, challenged, and/or have disabilities.

Culling resources from the school, home, and community, these counselors assist all students in developing self-understanding, responsibility, decision-making, and coping skills. Students are also aided in their efforts to develop values, attitudes, and skills required of productive citizens in a pluralistic society.

Crisis Intervention Advisor, Dean

The crisis intervention advisor or dean plays a pivotal role in helping students to self-actualize and to develop sufficient coping skills to enable them to acquire prudent attitudes and to make positive behavioral life decisions. In collaboration with teaching, Child Study Team, counseling, and medical and health staff, they promote and reinforce students' intellectual, emotional, and social growth and success.

They provide nonpunitive intervention and mediation, whenever possible.

A primary thrust in the performance of duties is to help students make the decision to productively and gainfully remain in school, through to completion.

Driver Education, Traffic Safety Personnel

The secondary school driver and traffic safety education program consists of both classroom and laboratory student-learning experiences. Personnel offering driver safety training help student motor vehicle operators to become safe and responsible street and highway users, and provide them with information about the overall highway transportation system.

In addition, they expose students to the social, financial, emotional, and physical responsibilities and challenges of licensed motor vehicle operators.

Health Care Advisor

The health education program should be an integral part of a health promotion program that assists students in developing the knowledge, attitudes, skills, and practices necessary to monitor, regulate, and ensure their health status.

Key to the performance of the health care advisor is the promotion of students' physical, emotional, and mental health.

As the goals, interests, and resources of the school and community permit, the health education program should include learning activities that provide for exploration of health occupations and preparation for initial entry into the health care delivery system.

Food Service Manager, Worker

Food service manager and workers supervise and engage in the preparation and serving of the food in school cafeterias and/or other school sites. They oversee and facilitate food preparation and cooking, check the quality of food and portion sizes, and ensure that dishes are prepared and delivered at the correct temperatures and, in a timely manner.

Point-of-service responsibility for cleaning and maintaining sanitary conditions, ensuring compliance with health and safety standards, are key job responsibilities.

In some instances, food service personnel monitor, or assist others to monitor, students during their in or out-of-class lunch period.

Head Custodian/Custodial Staff

The head custodian and custodial staff have responsibility for supervising and performing all tasks involved in the cleaning and maintenance of the school plant and/or grounds. Job specifications are varied, but consist primarily of ensuring that the physical plant is maintained up to sound health, safety, and aesthetic standards.

Preventative maintenance and repair are ongoing activities in order to ensure that the school physical environment is one in which staff and students can comfortably and safely function.

In-School Suspension Staff

In-school suspension is a placement that is used to remove the negative effects posed by disruptive students in the mainstream classroom. It offers a better option to out-of-school suspension when the need arises to exclude a student for behavioral infractions. In-school suspension staff is charged with maintaining an academic setting and ensuring that instructional services are provided to the assigned students. Along with facilitating students' academic growth, the staff strives to engage them in activities that promote positive behavioral changes, such as improved impulse control and effective coping skills.

The staff works with a changing population of students who serve varied lengths of time calculated on the basis of the severity of the infraction committed. In-school-suspension staff members collaborate with other school personnel to determine whether additional services will be required before the student is ready for successful reentry into the regular school program.

Paraprofessional, Teacher Aide, Teacher Assistant

The role of the paraprofessional or teacher aide is defined by the program to which he or she is assigned. The criteria for qualifying for the position are frequently dictated by the specific grade level and/or department in which he or she works.

Paraprofessionals are most often associated with the special education department, and work with a particular individual or group of students with learning and/or behavioral disabilities. Their work with students may include modifying materials, giving one-on-one assistance with specific tasks, helping monitor and control behaviors, and a range of other services, including those involving personal hygiene and mobility. They help ensure continuity of instruction, placing emphasis on promoting competence and maximizing independence of students requiring support.

Teacher aides' duties are those that support the teacher in order to facilitate the smooth delivery of instruction.

Teacher aides perform a wide range of tasks under the direct supervision of the classroom teacher.

The teacher assistant helps the classroom teacher to achieve goals and objectives for the delivery of instruction and to meet the needs of the whole child.

Helpful competencies in the performance of duties include the ability to relate to students and support their efforts to become self-reliant and to meet academic and other challenges posed on a day-to-day basis.

Duties are performed under the direct supervision of the classroom teacher.

Successful job performance is based on the demonstrated ability to assist the teacher without requiring ongoing direction and/or retraining.

Police Officer

The assigned police officer performs at the discretion of the school principal, and maintains ongoing communication and collaboration to determine where and when services are required.

During an assigned tour of duty, the officer patrols a designated area to provide assistance and protection for persons in the vicinity, safeguard property, assure the observance of the rules and regulations, apprehend violators, and provide support for the school security guard force.

The police officer possesses knowledge of the School Code of Conduct and Standard Policies and Procedures and performs all duties within the scope of their parameters.

Principal

The principal has the ultimate responsibility for all personnel and students, as well as the total operation of the school.

The job of principal is to maintain overall instructional and support operations at the assigned school; enforce school, district, and state policies; maintain the safety of the school environment; communicate information to staff; address situations, problems, and/or conflicts; develop school policies, vision, and mission goals; and guide the instructional program.

The principal's leadership is essential and evident in every phase of the daily school operation and is pivotal for facilitating short- and long-term planning in order to ensure that the needs of the educational community, staff, students, and parents are served.

School Attendance Counselor

The school attendance counselor has primary responsibility for determining the causes of student absenteeism or delinquency.

In close collaboration with the classroom teacher, parents, social services, and juvenile justice agencies, the attendance counselor searches for the root causes of the student's failure to attend school regularly.

When investigation indicates incidences of abuse, neglect, and/or need, the attendance counselor, in collaboration with the counseling and medical staff, undertakes action to bring needed services to the child, and, where indicated, to the family unit.

All efforts are geared toward the child receiving needed services and placement in a sound environment that is conducive to ongoing school attendance and general well-being.

School Nurse

Under the direction of the school principal, a physician, or other supervisory officer, the school nurse performs professional nursing duties pursuant to a school health program within a school district.

The nurse develops and maintains an in-depth knowledge of specific health needs and concerns of students and staff.

All prerequisite tests are conducted and student data are collected that are required to meet district and state health care mandates.

School Psychologist

In most instances, the school psychologist is an integral part of the school Child Study Team, although he or she may work independently or with a mental health agency and render diagnoses that are accepted by the school district.

The school psychologist is responsible for examining, classifying, and recommending a program of special education for pupils identified as having a handicap or disability, according to mandated state rules and regulations.

The psychologist may provide ongoing follow-up consultations and conduct tests for reevaluations, as mandated by the state.

Secretary, Supervisor Clerk, Clerk

The school secretary takes care of administrative details, schedules appointments, and handles school communication, interacting with parents and the community members concerning school news and events.

The secretary occupies an important position in the school organization and is often the first person to interact with the public when they are engaging in school-related business.

Working alone, or in concert with other clerical staff, the school secretary performs a myriad of tasks that sustains the fundamental operation of the school in an efficient and productive manner.

Security Guard

Under the direction of the principal, the school security guard patrols the school plant and grounds, providing protection from harm to persons and property; and remains vigilant against fire, theft, vandalism, illegal or unauthorized entry, and any and all disruption to the safe and orderly functioning of the school.

In many instances, members of the school security force are assigned to specific posts, and as a result, become familiar with the staff and students who work within their jurisdiction, along with the schedules, activities, and procedures that are engaged in within those specific areas.

As special assignments, school security guards often provide services during off-site school activities, such as sports events, field trips, etc.

School security guards uphold the School Code of Conduct, District Policies and Procedures, and collaborate with the assigned building police officers.

**CORWIN
PRESS**

The Corwin Press logo—a raven striding across an open book—represents the union of courage and learning. Corwin Press is committed to improving education for all learners by publishing books and other professional development resources for those serving the field of K–12 education. By providing practical, hands-on materials, Corwin Press continues to carry out the promise of its motto: "**Helping Educators Do Their Work Better.**"